# Flight From Dallas

New Evidence of CIA Involvement in the Murder of President John F. Kennedy

by

**James P. Johnston
& Jon Roe**

Order this book online at www.trafford.com
or email orders@trafford.com

Most Trafford titles are also available at major online book retailers.

© Copyright 2007 James P. Johnston & Jon Roe.

All rights reserved. No part of this publication may be reproduced, stored in a retrieval system, or transmitted, in any form or by any means, electronic, mechanical, photocopying, recording, or otherwise, without the written prior permission of the author.

Print information available on the last page.

ISBN: 978-1-4120-7236-6 (sc)
ISBN: 978-1-4122-0631-0 (e)

Because of the dynamic nature of the Internet, any web addresses or links contained in this book may have changed since publication and may no longer be valid. The views expressed in this work are solely those of the author and do not necessarily reflect the views of the publisher, and the publisher hereby disclaims any responsibility for them.

Any people depicted in stock imagery provided by Thinkstock are models, and such images are being used for illustrative purposes only. Certain stock imagery © Thinkstock.

*Trafford rev. 06/01/2015*

   www.trafford.com

**North America & international**
toll-free: 1 888 232 4444 (USA & Canada)
fax: 812 355 4082

# CONTENTS

List Of Illustrations ................................................................... v
Acknowledgments .................................................................. vii
Chapter 1: A Patriot's Questions ............................................... 1
Chapter 2: Learning to Do His Duty .......................................... 3
Chapter 3: Problems for a President and a Sergeant ................ 16
Chapter 4: The Flight ............................................................... 22
Chapter 5: Enter the CIA ......................................................... 30
Chapter 6: Working for 'The Agency' ...................................... 66
Chapter 7: Finding an Ally ....................................................... 76
Chapter 8: Finding Answers ..................................................... 87
Chapter 9: The Scenario of an Assassination ......................... 103
Chapter 10: A Patriot's Questions .......................................... 106
Index ...................................................................................... 109

# LIST OF ILLUSTRATIONS

1. Robert G. Vinson today ............................................................. 39
2. Seventeen year old soldier Bob Vinson........................... 40
3. Vinson with class in Okinawa at the school he and his squadron adopted...................................................................... 41
4. Bob and Bobbie Vinson in the 1960's............................ 42
5. Carl Vinson............................................................................. 43
6. Fred Vinson............................................................................ 44
7. Vinson receives NCO of the Month at NORAD ............. 45-46
8. Vinson receives the Joint Service Commendation Medal..... 47
9. Vinson receives his sergeant's stripes .............................. 48
10. A Douglas C-54, the type of airplane that made the flight to and out of Dallas................................................................... 49
11. Map locating where the plane landed in Dallas ................ 50
12. Aerial photo of the landing site taken January 4, 1964 ........ 51
13. Vinson's orders to report to Arlington, VA ...................... 53
14. Vinson's orders to report to Las Vegas ........................... 54
15. Map depicting Site 51 where Vinson was stationed by CIA. 55
16. Vinson's Retirement Order ................................................. 56
17. Vinson receives Small Business Administration C Counseling Certificate................................................................ 57
18. Curriculum Vitae of James S. Sobek, P.E...................... 61
19. CIA Freedom of Information Act response proving Vinson's presence at CIA headquarters in Langley, VA ................ 63
20. FBI correspondence refusing investigation ...................... 65

# ACKNOWLEDGMENTS

The authors wish to acknowledge the contributions to this book of the following persons and especially to Colleen Kelly Johnston for her laborious preparation of the Index and proofing the manuscript. Also to Robert G. Vinson for his courage and belief that the facts of the assassination of Pres. John F. Kennedy must continue to be told.

Special thanks to Richard McCabe for his efforts in obtaining flight information and specifications of the Douglas C-54 from the Douglas Archives at Santa Monica, California.

Casey Johnston-Sloan, Hugh Kelly, Carl Williams, Patrick Pippin, R.P.L.S., Cathy Brewer, James S. Sobek, P.E., William E. Hendrix, MAJ USAF Ret., Richard Walkup, Kerry J. Johnston, Larry Hatteberg and John Judge.

# Chapter 1
# A Patriot's Questions

It swoops down on him when he least expects it. When he's carrying groceries into the house or watching a movie on television, sitting at the scoring table waiting for his turn to bowl or looking through antique stores with his wife. Then he remembers.

Suddenly what's in front of him -- the comfortable, every day duties of retirement -- are replaced by the four-engine rumble of a C-54 and the sudden midair correction that transports him into the heart of a nation's tragedy. The white short-sleeved shirt with three pens in the pocket becomes starched khaki, his white and blue running shoes turn to black Air Force issue. He is once again a 34-year old sergeant wanting only to get home to Colorado Springs, but instead landing in Dallas, where he looks across the airplane's cabin into the face of...

But it can't be. He couldn't have seen who he saw. And the face across from him turns back into the sales clerk or the gas station attendant, and the memory disappears just as everyone and everything disappeared that night. Disappeared and left him sitting on a runway in New Mexico in the middle of a mystery that is as crisp, clear, yet impenetrable as the day it happened -- November 22, 1963. Everyone and everything but the memory and the questions and the knowledge that he was involved in the crime of the century.

Lately, as the number of people who can provide answers to his questions decreases, he feels time running out. But you'd never know it to look at him. Robert Vinson isn't a man given to panic and histrionics. Quiet, soft-spoken, he chooses his words with the care he puts into cleaning the windshield of his Dodge Minivan when he fills it with gas on trips he and his wife take to visit their grandkids. He waits to speak, lets others go first. He's waited a long time now. And when he finally spoke, he found there's no record anywhere of that harrowing flight.

According to all the existing records, it never happened.

But Bob Vinson knows it did. And he also knows time is running out. Twice retired -- after 20 years in the U.S. Air Force and 20 in city administration -- he spends his days relaxing, reading history, shopping with Roberta in their Florida retirement community. It's the life Americans strive toward, the rewards of working hard, living right, saving up, planning well. He's given his country a lifetime of service. In return, he lives in comfortable, quiet retirement. But he wants more. He wants answers, starting with who were the men who accompanied him that day in 1963, and what was their mission?

To understand the seriousness of the man and his questions, you need to understand his life up to November 22, 1963, the life of one who never made waves, didn't ask questions and didn't have grave doubts about his government. A man who never dreamt anything could happen that would be as strange, as disquieting, as frightening in its consequences as that flight to and from Dallas.

# Chapter 2

# Learning to Do His Duty

He always had a job, and he always worked hard at it, not complaining or demanding. He did his duty. It was a way of life.

Robert Griel Vinson was born December 12, 1928, in Headland, Alabama, the seventh of 10 children of Robert Griel Vinson and Effie Katy Rebecca Anna McCall, pious, hard workers, who somehow kept all of their children fed, clothed, educated and on the straight and narrow.

His mother rose at 5 A.M. prepared breakfast, cleaned the kitchen, then went out to help in the fields. She read the Bible every day, made sure her children lived by the Ten Commandments and attended Sunday School.

His father was excellent at math, and helped his children with their home work, even though he had only a sixth grade education. He was an ace mechanic and after he married Effie, he left the family farm to work for an auto repair shop in Headland, where he soon gained a reputation as the best mechanic in Southeast Alabama. By 1925, he and his brother, Zemer, had opened their own repair shop.

Bob was born three years later, and grew up fascinated by family stories about his great grandmother being a full-blooded Creek Native American, and about relatives throughout the south. His father talked about the Vinson cousins just across the state line in Georgia. The George Vinson family produced Carl -- powerful chairman of the House Armed Services Committee, and the longest serving member of Congress -- and Chief Justice of the Supreme Court Fred Vinson. That Vinson family would later move to Kentucky. But it appeared early on that Bob Vinson would never travel far from Headland.

The auto repair shop of his father and uncle was booming when he was born in '28. In fact, the partners had invested much of their profits in real estate. Then the Depression hit, and by 1931 -- when far to the north, 14 year old John Kennedy began his finishing school education at Choate School in Wallington, Conn. -- the Vinson partners were struggling. By 1932, they were wiped out.

Robert Vinson gave his half of the partnership to his brother, and moved his brood back to the farm 60 miles away in Coffee County. Times may have been tough, but four year old Bobby thrived amidst the pigs, chickens, goats, mules, cows and his dog, Snooks, who was an expert rattlesnake killer until one day when one of them got him first. Snook's death was one of the few sad days Bobby experienced on the farm, where -- spending the entire day with his father -- he learned the work habits of his life.

By 1936 -- the year John Kennedy, the Choate graduate named "most likely to succeed," entered Harvard -- eight-year old Bob was driving two mules on a wagon loaded with a bale of cotton to the town gin mill to separate out the seed for next year's planting. During the summer, he'd drive a wagon loaded with cut wood to Enterprise, Alabama, and sell it for $2.00. And when his dad butchered a hog, Bob would take it to town to sell by the piece, getting as much as $2.00 for the whole ham. The money bought family staples such as salt, pepper, sugar and flour.

When Bob was 10, his father traded a sow and two pigs for a Model T Ford. They cut out the rumble seat and built a bed on the back. This allowed them to haul vegetables from their five-acre garden to town to sell door to door, earning money to buy clothes, tea for Sunday and new shoes each year. That same year, John F. Kennedy arrived in London to begin a European research tour for his senior honors thesis on Great Britain's lack of preparation for the approaching war.

And two years later, when Kennedy's *Why England Slept* was published to rave reviews, the Vinsons bought a one and a half ton truck without a cab or bed. They bought a cab at a junkyard and built a flatbed that allowed them to increase what they hauled to three bales of cotton or three tons of peanuts. Bob was soon hauling for other farmers in the area as well.

The war in Europe began September 1, 1939, and Bob's older brothers joined the service or took war-related jobs in the cities. At 12 years of age, Bob had to quit school to run the farm. That same year John F. Kennedy graduated *cum laude* from Harvard.

Running the farm proved too much for a teenager, and in 1942, the Vinsons gave it up, moving to Lockhart, Alabama, where Bob's father worked as a mechanic for McDaniel Motor Co., the Chevrolet dealership in nearby Florala, Alabama. When a new Ford dealership came to town, he was offered a 40 percent partnership, and Bob was given an evening job there as a mechanic.

He went to Lockhart Junior High and played basketball there for two years. But, it was a difficult adjustment, since he was three years older than his fellow students, and he decided to quit school and work fulltime for $28 a week.

During Bob's junior high school years, Jack Kennedy was turned down for service in the U.S. Army, accepted by the Navy, and August 2, 1943 the PT boat he commanded -- PT109 -- was rammed and sunk by a Japanese destroyer. Kennedy rescued crew members, and was awarded the Purple Heart and the Navy and Marine Corps Medal.

In 1946, Bob was drinking a milk shake during lunch at Florala's downtown drug store, talking with his friend, soda jerk Gorman Lindsey. An Army recruiting officer walked by the store.

"Bob, would you join the Army if I did?" Gorman asked.

"Sure."

It was as simple as that. He vaguely knew that the Army offered opportunities for education and a career, but then -- for the Alabama boy who'd just turned 17 -- the Army represented more than anything else, the opportunity to see some of the world beyond Alabama.

The two took the written exam in the trailer where the recruiter had parked, and were told to meet him there at 3:00 P.M. with bags packed and the signatures of their fathers on the enlistment papers.

Bob hurried home, packed his clothes and waited for his mother to wash three pair of underwear so he'd have enough. Then he gave her a hug goodbye and went back to the garage to get his father's signature. But his father wouldn't sign. And he wouldn't say why. Bob was shattered, stymied. Suddenly all his dreams had coalesced in the Army, and just as suddenly, the man he respected more than any other had dashed them. He was hurt and frustrated, but he didn't for a moment blame his father. Although the two never discussed it, today he believes he understands that his father simply couldn't let go of the youngest boy of the family, the one to whom he was closest.

For Bob, the demarcation line between youth and adulthood had never seemed clearer. He had the next few minutes to determine the direction his life would take. And he did something he had never imagined. He went behind his father's back. His older brother, William -- who was parts manager at the same Ford dealership -- listened to his plea and nodded.

"Yeah, that'd be a good place for you to finish up your education," he said, and forged their father's name on the papers.

At 3:00 that afternoon, Bob arrived at the recruiting trailer. Gorman didn't.

Even alone, without the slightest idea of where he would go or what he would encounter, Bob went through with it, driving with the recruiter 80 miles to Pensacola. They stopped at a neighborhood bar, where the teetotaler had his first two beers and Pensacola got a little blurry and tilted. That night he tried to eat a steak cooked by the recruiter's wife, but couldn't get it down and, around 8:00 P.M., he was on a Greyhound Bus sleeping fitfully for most of the 12 hours it took to get to Atlanta, Georgia.

May 10, 1946, Bob and some 50 other young men were sworn into the United States Army. The next day they were issued their gear and the day after that, boarded a troop train that traveled for two days, then pulled onto a side track where they sat through another day. Finally, at 7:00 P.M., trucks arrived and took them to Camp Polk,

Louisiana. At 5:00 A.M., the next morning, they began eight weeks of basic training. But Bob didn't do the full eight weeks.

Two officers from North Camp Polk showed up six weeks into training and told him to pack his bags and go with them. At North Camp Polk they showed him two small spotter planes, that looked like 1946 Cessnas modified to hold a stretcher behind the pilot and copilot seats. The planes were used to take soldiers to Barksdale Air Force Base in Louisiana for medical treatment. Since he'd scored high on his aptitude tests and had auto mechanic experience, he'd been chosen to service those aircraft, and bypass the final two weeks of basic training.

One of the officers showed Bob around the base, and he went to work maintaining the aircraft. He earned $25 a month and had $22 deducted and sent to his mother. With all the other deductions, his first paycheck was for 10 cents. Bob bought a Coke and a candy bar. But after a couple of months of 10 cent paydays, he decided he had to do something. He wrote his mother, asking her to send him $5. She sent him $2. He used the money to buy a big box of chocolates, which he put in his locker. And -- after hours -- whenever anyone wanted a piece of candy, they came to Bob, paying a nickel a piece. He kept that business going for a long while and through several boxes of chocolates.

Only a few days after Bob had started his duties, one of the lieutenants told him he and his fellow officer had received orders to leave immediately.

"What am I supposed to do?" Bob asked.

"I don't know," he said. "Just keep reporting here each morning until someone tells you differently."

And he did, doing his job each day with no supervision or supervisors.

That same year -- June 24, 1946 -- Secretary of the Treasury Frederick Moore Vinson, 56-year old Kentuckian, and cousin of Bob, was appointed chief justice of the U.S. Supreme Court by President Truman. And, recovered from his war wounds and having worked briefly as a reporter for Hearst newspapers, John F. Kennedy was elected to Congress from Massachusetts' 11th Congressional District.

Nearly five months after Bob started working on the two aircraft, a sergeant showed up and told him to report to a major in the orderly room. The major was furious. Why hadn't the private reported to him before this? Bob told him what the lieutenant had told him. The major stared at him for a minute, then snapped, "OK," and gave him his new assignment. He'd make coffee every day in the Mess Hall.

So Bob went from airplane mechanic to coffee brewer, and never complained. This was, he was learning, the way the army operated. He was good at taking orders and good at getting the job done. And he brewed a fine vat of coffee.

But the coffee brewing job lasted only three weeks until the Army closed Camp Polk on December 22 and the troops boarded a train that took them to Fort Dix, New Jersey.

It was Christmas Eve, 1946, when Bob stumbled off the troop train, was given two blankets and assigned to a barracks with no heat. It was the farthest from home he'd ever been, his first time north, and he froze. And the day after Christmas, when they fell out for roll call, he saw his first snow. That was the day Bob got his next assignment -- he was in charge of the mail room. And, although he knew nothing about operating a mail room, he was delighted to be working indoors.

In March of 1947, he was given orders to report to Camp Kilmer, New Jersey. There, he was promoted to T/4 and put in charge of making sure all mustering out pay was sent to soldiers returning from overseas -- $300 in three payments. He was sending out more than 3,000 checks a day. That May he met Helen Mary Penrose, whom he married November 10th. Two days later, he was discharged from the U.S. Army. He and Helen set off for home, where Bob planned to open his own auto repair shop. Nothing could have been further from his life and of less interest than the debate that raged that year over the establishment of a new unit of government occasioned by the Cold War.

In that year of 1947, as the Cold War with the Soviet Union developed, President Truman established an agency that would coordinate information gathered in a variety of ways about nations around the world. The object of this process was to insure that the President received clear and concise reports that could be confirmed and put into a global context.

But there was opposition to Truman's plan, particularly from young Republican Allen Dulles, who in a memo to the Senate Armed Services Committee argued that much more than "coordination" was needed. "Intelligence work in terms of people will require other techniques, other personnel, and will have rather different objectives," he wrote, "We must deal with the problem of conflicting ideologies as democracy faces communism, not only in the relations between Soviet Russia and the countries of the East, but in the international political conflicts with the countries of Europe, Asia and South America." Dulles and others wanted more -- much more -- than an information-gathering agency. And it was he who contributed to the eventual law a clause enabling the agency to carry out "such other functions and duties related to intelligence as the National Security Council may from time to time direct". [1]

That one clause would give birth to one of the most powerful, deadly and secret agencies ever devised. They called it the Central Intelligence Agency.

Home in Lockhart, Alabama, Bob got a reminder of how rough things had been before he joined the army. They were still rough. He couldn't borrow the money to open his repair shop, and he couldn't find a mechanic's job. So, he earned $80 a month working as a sacker at the grocery store and $90 from service in the U.S. Government Training Program. Things didn't get better, and on March 17, 1948, he went to where he knew he'd get a break -- back to the military service.

But he had to take a reduction in rank from T/4 to Corporal, since he'd waited too long to reenlist. Another difference -- rather than returning to the Army, he joined the Air Force mainly because he was told he would be stationed in the repair and maintenance section at nearby Eglin Air Force Base in Florida, which was like staying in his home neighborhood.

It was the military service that had gotten Bob out of the back country of Alabama two years earlier. Now it was the service that allowed him to come home, yet rescued him from the financial hardships he found there.

Later that year, New York Governor Thomas Dewey and California Governor Earl Warren lost the presidential, vice-presidential election to Harry Truman and Alben W. Barkley. Allen Dulles had served as a speechwriter in the Republican's losing cause. When it looked like they'd win, Dewey promised Dulles he'd make him director of the new CIA. [2] Dulles may have worked in a losing cause, but he didn't forget the promise.

In December, Bob was recruited by Major James W. Johnson to join him in the Forestry Division of Eglin Air Force Base Reservation. The job offered a variety of duties, everything from typing to patrolling the reservation, fighting forest fires to building fish ponds.

The very next day, Bob reported to his new assignment, along with Helen and their daughters, Angela and Dolores. In addition to all the other duties, he was assigned as an extra in the film *Twelve O'Clock High*, which turned the base into a 1942 British air base from which Gregory Peck commanded bombing raids into Germany. Another additional duty at Eglin turned out to be a lifetime blessing -- education.

"I had only an eighth grade education when I joined the army", Vinson recalls. "So I started attending high school at night in Crestview, Florida. Major Johnson didn't have any kids, and kind of adopted me. He assigned my civil service co-worker, Noah Corbin, to see to it that I spent no less than two hours a day studying. I worked for Major Johnson from December, 1948 to February 1951, and I give him the credit for my education and my desire to continue it throughout my life."

Since that day in '48, Vinson would receive his General Education Development (GED) diploma, complete work in three in-service institutes, compile 130 hours in eight U.S. universities and receive his BA degree in Business Administration from Kansas Newman College in Wichita, Kansas.

Bob re-enlisted in 1951, launching a busy four-year stint that took him to Eniwetok Island, where he was postal supervisor when the first hydrogen bomb was tested there. Then came service in Okinawa, where he won a commendation for his contributions to a school his 51st Civil Engineering Squadron adopted there. He supervised construction of a playground, wiring of the building for electricity and a full day's field trip for the kids to the air base. All money was donated by the soldiers and all work was done on off-duty time.

On duty in Japan, he found himself doing undercover work for the captain, reporting on drug trafficking and racketeering at the base.

In 1953, he came back to the States, as base recruiter at Oxnard, California, then transferred to Washington D.C. in July of '54, where he researched Air Force security clearances.

Meanwhile, in 1952, John Kennedy had been elected to the US Senate and Dwight D. Eisenhower and Earl W. Warren had made a deal. In return for his help at the Republican national convention, the

California governor was promised by Eisenhower the first available Supreme Court seat. That seat came open when Chief Justice Fred Vinson died in 1953 and -- even though Eisenhower argued he'd promised him a seat, but not the chief justice's seat -- Warren wouldn't back down. Eisenhower told him he could have the job if he'd leave the California governor's job and report to the court in time for the opening of the new term in just seven days. Eisenhower thought he wouldn't do it. Warren did it.[3]

That same year, Eisenhower also kept the five-year old promise of Thomas Dewey, and appointed Allen Dulles director of the CIA.

That was also the year John Kennedy and Jacqueline Bouvier were married.

In 1954, Bob re-enlisted and, for the first time in years, spent the next three years in one place, serving as an Air Force recruiter in Baltimore, Maryland.

In 1955, *Profiles in Courage* by John F. Kennedy won the Pulitzer Prize. The next year, the senator barely missed in an attempt to win the Democratic vice-presidential nomination. And, in 1957, Senator Kennedy was appointed to the powerful Senate Foreign Relations Committee. The same year, at age 40, he became the father of a baby girl, Caroline.

Bob's marriage to Helen broke up during duty in Amarillo, Texas. On December 18, 1959, he married widow Roberta Bolin Huddleston, and became stepfather to a son Benton and daughter Sandra.

That same year, President Eisenhower and CIA Director Dulles laid the cornerstone at the new CIA headquarters in Langley,

Virginia. Dulles had been telling the President that Cuba was a danger to the United States and that its leader, Fidel Castro, was not supported by the majority of the populace. He wanted the U.S. to invade and overthrow Castro. In March, 1960, Eisenhower gave approval to start recruiting and training Cuban refugees for an invasion. Intelligence officers were never told of the plan and thus were never able to analyze chances for success.[4]

Bob was transferred from Amarillo, Texas to Naha AFB, Okinawa, where he served as first sergeant of the 51$^{st}$ Civil Engineering Squadron. He also attended the Non-Commissioned Officer's Air Academy at Kadena AFB there.

His career continued to blossom. As, of course, did that of John F. Kennedy.

# Chapter 3

# Problems for a President and a Sergeant

*The new frontier is here, whether we seek it or not. Beyond that frontier are the uncharted areas of science and space, unsolved problems of peace and war, unconquered pockets of ignorance and prejudice, unanswered questions of poverty and surplus. It would be easier to shrink back from that frontier, to look to the safe mediocrity of the past, to be lulled by good intentions and high rhetoric -- and those who prefer that course should not cast their votes for me, regardless of party.*

Bob leaned forward on the couch. Like most Americans he didn't know much about the thin young man giving the speech. But like many Americans that July 15, 1960, he liked what he heard.

*For courage and not complacency is our need today. Leadership, not salesmanship. And the only valid test of leadership is the ability to lead, and to lead vigorously.*

John Kennedy's acceptance speech at the Los Angeles Democratic convention made a deep impression on the young Air Force man who watched it on television. He liked the courage and determination of the man. And as the presidential campaign continued, he liked what he heard as Kennedy outlined many of the themes that would be addressed in his presidency.

*Our problems are man-made, therefore they may be solved by man. No problem of human destiny is beyond human beings.*

*Let us think of education as the means of developing our greatest abilities, because in each of us there is a private hope and dream which, fulfilled, can be translated into benefit for everyone and greater strength for our nation.*

*...(L)et us strive to build peace, a desire for peace, a willingness to work for peace in the hearts and minds of all our people. I believe that we can. I believe the problems of human destiny are not beyond the reach of human beings.*

Bob was inspired by Kennedy's words, and cast one of the votes that put the first member of his generation, and the father of a new baby boy -- John Jr. -- in the White House.

But the early-going proved rough for Kennedy, largely because of the failed CIA-planned and executed Bay of Pigs invasion of Cuba, April 17, 1961. The CIA blamed the debacle on the president for not providing air support, even though Kennedy had not promised it and had insisted that the U.S. military was not to be used. The president -- who publically took the blame -- privately blamed the CIA for devising such a vainglorious, and patently impossible scheme, and lying to administration members about its feasibility. His wish, Kennedy said, was "to splinter the CIA into a thousand pieces and scatter it to the winds." [5]

June 1, 1961, Kennedy prepared to transfer clandestine operations from the CIA to the Joint Chiefs of Staff, and by year's end, he'd fired all the agency's top covert operators and its director, Allen Dulles.[6]

By 1963, Kennedy had signed the historic nuclear test ban treaty and, turned to what he considered another no-win situation. In Southeast Asia -- as in Cuba -- the CIA had drawn the United States deeper into a situation that could now be won only through massive and costly US military involvement. After Laos was neutralized through diplomatic efforts, Vietnam became the major focus of Kennedy's attention in Southeast Asia. Not to be hoodwinked twice, Kennedy told aides: "The first thing I do when I'm re-elected, I'm going to get the Americans out of Vietnam." October 2, 1963, the President approved National Security Act Memorandum #263, which "plans to withdraw 1,000 US military personnel by the end of 1963...(E)ssential functions now performed by the US military personnel can be carried out by Vietnamese by the end of 1965. It should be possible to withdraw the bulk of US personnel by that time."[7] A report in the New York Times November 21, 1963 reiterated Kennedy's intention.[8]

Political considerations were breaking out everywhere a year before the next presidential election. Vice President Lyndon Johnson's top aide Bobby Baker had left the government under an influence peddling scandal that would undoubtedly be part of the Republican attack in 1964, and rumors were rife that Kennedy planned to drop Johnson from the ticket, in fact had already offered the number two spot to his good friend, Florida Sen. George Smathers.[9]

And now there was a party split in Texas that demanded a presidential visit to calm roiling political waters brimming with something more, something the young president had met more than enough of in recent years. The atmosphere in Texas in 1963 was one of hatred.

Suddenly, things weren't going well for Bob Vinson either.

He and Roberta (whom he called Bobbie) had moved to Colorado Springs, where he was was administrative supervisor for the electronics division, North American Air Defense Command (NORAD) at Ent Air Force Base. They loved living there. But Bob felt it was past time for his next promotion. Particularly since -- as first sergeant of the 51st Civil Engineering Squadron -- he had received outstanding performance evaluations, the PACAF Achievement Certificate and a letter of commendation from his commanding officer stating that he should be promoted at the earliest possible date. But even though he held important jobs, did them all with dispatch, studied and passed all the tests, went before the promotion boards and met all the requirements, it never came. He watched others get the promotions that he felt he had earned. He asked everyone why, and was told: "We don't know why. We don't have access to all the records." His superior officers had given him superior ratings. But they also referred to him in more than one of those evaluations as mild-mannered, easy to get along with, not one to make waves.

Maybe, Bob felt, it was wave-making time. Always before, Bob Vinson had simply done his work and been rewarded. Now, something had gone wrong, and waiting was no longer working. He talked it over with Bobbie, seemingly endlessly, and the two of them decided that for the first time in his career, he would not quietly do his job. He would go by the book, but go over his superiors' heads. He would request a week's leave of absence, fly to Washington, and meet with those in the Pentagon who could review his records and tell him -- and his superior officers -- whether he was deserving of a promotion. Something was wrong, and he decided he had to try to fix it.

So, on November 20 -- while John Kennedy was preparing to fly to Dallas to fix a problem -- Robert Vinson flew to Washington, D.C., to deal with a problem of his own. He would soon find himself in the middle of the mystery of the century.

He arrived in the nation's capitol on a cool, brisk evening, got a hotel downtown and the next morning walked to the Capitol. But his first stop wasn't business. It was a courtesy call to one of his heroes -- Representative Carl Vinson, brother of the late Fred Vinson, head of the powerful House Armed Services Committee and Bob's distant cousin. The two had a good chat about Georgia and Alabama and about how they were both pretty sure they were related.

Then Bob went to the Capitol basement office of a Col. Chapman, liaison officer between Congress and the Pentagon. Sometime between one and two o'clock, Bob was sitting across Chapman's desk in his Capitol basement office. The colonel received a phone call, and told the caller:

"We have information, and I strongly recommend that the president not go to Dallas." He said that even though the advance group of congressmen had already left for Texas, he still urged that the president not make the trip.

Obviously rebuffed by his caller, the upset colonel hung up the phone, and turned back to Bob's records. Quickly, he sent Bob in a limousine to the Pentagon, where a personnel officer and then a senior master sergeant interviewed him and looked over his records. The sergeant took them into a colonel's office and about 20 minutes later, Bob was summoned into the office where the colonel told him they'd look into it. Bob waited a few more minutes before the sergeant returned his file, and said: "We don't understand why you've been passed over. We'll take care of it."

Business completed, Bob went back to the hotel, had dinner, called Bobbie with the good news and told her that first thing Friday morning he'd catch the regular shuttle plane from Andrews Air Force Base to Ent at Colorado Springs. Air Force personnel, who were in uniform and had proper papers, hitched free rides to their home bases on military aircraft headed their way. And every Friday and Wednesday, a shuttle went out of Andrews bound for Colorado Springs.

It had a been a productive day, and Bob slept well. The next morning he would begin what would become the longest, most mysterious and most unforgettable day of his life.

# Chapter 4

# The Flight

Bob caught an early bus, and arrived at Andrews at 7:30 the morning of November 22nd. Inside the passenger terminal, he approached an airman at the check-in desk, wrote his name on the check-in sheet, and asked if any flights were scheduled out that morning for Denver or Colorado Springs. The airman said, no, there were no flights at all out of Andrews that day.

That struck Bob as very strange, given the regular shuttle flights to Ent on Wednesdays and Fridays. He'd never known one of them to be canceled.

"Are you sure?"

"Yeah. We don't have a thing going."

This could develop into a long wait. And Bob hadn't had breakfast. So, he told the airman he was going to the restaurant across the hall, and if anything unscheduled came up, to let him know. The waitress had just brought Bob's bacon, eggs and biscuit, when he was paged over the airport intercom. He took two bites, paid his bill and hurried back to the counter.

"You got something going out?" he said at the counter.

"Oh, yes," said the airman. "You see that C-54 out there?"

He turned and peered out onto the sun-dappled runway. "You mean the third one down there?"

"Yeah. Go get on it. It's going to Denver, Lowry Air Force Base."

"OK! Thanks!" He grabbed his bag and rushed out to the airplane. But there seemed no need to rush. There was only one person with the plane, walking around under it, apparently doing a pre-flight inspection. Bob noticed that the man was in olive drab coveralls that bore no insignia or markings of any kind. That was strange for an Air Force Base. And even stranger was the aircraft. The large plane, with its nose wheel and four propeller-driven engines, was a familiar one to Bob, as it was to almost anyone who'd spent any time around aircraft. Constructed by Douglas Aircraft during the late 1930s for American, Eastern and United Airlines, it was caught in the draft. By the time it was certified, all transport aircraft in production were diverted to the armed forces. During the war, and until production ceased in August, 1947, 1,163 were built, and in peacetime the plane became the standard craft on U.S. airlines. But by 1963, they were being phased out, and this plane was one of the few hundred that had not yet been modified into freight carriers.

Yes, it was a very familiar plane, except for one thing. It carried no markings...except for an emblem on its tail that appeared to be a graphic of the earth, rust brown with white grid marks on it separating latitude and longitude. At Air Force bases, the planes all had "USAF" and serial numbers printed on their tails.

Not this one.

The door was open and steps led into it, so Bob climbed aboard. The plane was empty. No passengers. No freight. The man in coveralls ignored him. He settled into a seat over the wings, where he'd been told is the safest place to sit. He was on the right side, looking out the front of the plane. He watched as a second man in unmarked coveralls joined the first in checking out the aircraft. He remembers the two as Caucasians of medium build, one about 5-9, 165 to 180 pounds, the other about 5-11 and 160 pounds. There were no distinguishing characteristics. Neither wore a hat or cap. They boarded the plane, saying nothing to him, not even nodding hello, and disappeared into the cockpit.

Things were getting stranger by the minute. No one asked Bob to sign his name on a manifest, an Air Force requirement. Generally the pilot would welcome a passenger aboard, ask where he was headed, talk about the flight and the weather. And there was no crew chief, another Air Force requirement. He saw no flight log. The pilot on such flights always carried a brief case with maps and such. The two men in coveralls carried nothing as they climbed aboard the plane, shut the hatch and pulled the cockpit door shut behind them. The engines roared, and the plane taxied down the runway. The few clouds that had filtered the early morning sun were gone now, and bright sunlight greeted the takeoff between 8:30 and 9 (Eastern Standard Time). The plane headed west, reaching the average cruising speed of 170 miles per hour. Bob looked out the window at the land rolling by beneath him. There was silence from the crew until somewhere over Nebraska at around 12:30, one of the two men in the cockpit announced in a flat, unemotional voice over the loudspeaker that the president had been shot at 12:29.

That's all he said.

But immediately after that announcement, the plane made a sharp 90-degree turn. It was no longer headed west, but south. Bob watched in consternation as an Air Force base with B-29s on the tarmac drifted by below. The B-29s were kept at Offett AFB in Omaha at that time. The southerly course continued. Then, sometime between 3:30 and 4:00 P.M., Central Standard Time, he saw a familiar sight out the window. He'd seen it many times before as he and Roberta had come up from Amarillo and down from Colorado Springs to visit his stepson, Benton, and his two grandsons.

They were over Dallas.

Dallas and the assassination didn't click in Bob's mind. For one thing, he didn't know if the president was in Dallas, especially since he'd heard the colonel urge that he not go.

Coming over the city from the northwest, the plane landed on an area of sand inside the city limits, close to downtown just south of the Trinity River in the floodplain. There was no runway. The area looked more like a road under construction than anything else. The plane made a very rough landing, and Bob saw that they were on what looked like a big sand bar. There seemed to be low white cliffs to the south and a tool shed that he supposed to be four by six feet in size, the kind of shed highway construction crews used. There was no equipment, just a jeep with the top down -- yellow with no insignia. The river and some scrub trees to the north and, behind them, the city skyline.

Two men jumped from the jeep and ran to the airplane. The jeep backed up and out of Bob's sight. With the engines still running, one of the crew came out of the cockpit to unhinge and shove open the passenger door so the two men could board the plane. They wore offwhite, beige coveralls such as those worn by repairmen who work on streets, highways or sewers. The taller of the two -- a Latino, Bob took him to be Cuban -- shut and locked the door. He stood 6 feet to 6-1 and weighed between 180 and 190. The shorter one, a Caucasian, was 5-7 to 5-9, weighing 150 to 160. The two walked past Bob without a word or a look, and took seats up front right behind the cockpit.

They didn't say a word, to him or to each other.

The plane taxied for a few yards, then turned and -- about 15 minutes after it set down -- took off headed northwest, the way it had landed.

Obviously, Bob thought, they were following orders. They knew what they were doing, and didn't have to explain anything to him. He was just hitching a ride. Besides, they were no doubt upset by the fact that the president had been shot. So was he. It wasn't a time to be bothering strangers asking questions. So he kept quiet too. Around dusk, the plane landed again and taxied to the edge of a runway. But they weren't in Denver's Lowry. Bob didn't recognize the air base.

The cockpit door opened, and the two crewman came barreling down the aisle. The two passengers followed. Without a word, or even a look at him, they rushed past him and out the door of the plane. He watched them disappear into the darkness of the seemingly deserted base.

Were they coming back to go on to Denver? Why were they in such a rush? Where were they? Bob Vinson sat there a few moments trying to make sense of the strangest flight of his life.

Then, he decided he'd better get some answers.

He descended from the plane and stood alone on the runway, the darkness closing in around him. Even though it was only about 6:30 in the evening, the place was deserted. The only light came from a building across the runway, and he walked toward it. Inside, he found an Air Policeman behind a counter. Not another soul was in sight.

"Hi," Bob said. "Can you tell me where I am?"

"You're at Roswell Air Force Base in New Mexico," the AP said.

Roswell, UFO Capitol of the World, where unidentified flying objects had been sighted again and again, and where -- Bob was later to learn -- the CIA had a secret base. He didn't know any of this back then.

"I thought I was going to Denver, Colorado."

"No, you're at Roswell."

"Well, I guess this is as far as my ride's going. How can I get downtown and catch a bus?"

"You can't go anywhere right how."

"Why? What's the matter?"

"This base is under full alert and nobody can leave or enter."

"But we just landed."

"Well, I don't know anything about that. But you can't leave until the alert is lifted."

He motioned to some chairs in the waiting room, and Bob sat and waited, once more going over the crazy day in his mind. He noted that the AP at a base on full alert saw him get off an incoming airplane and didn't even ask his name, let alone ask who his fellow passengers were or to where they had disappeared.

Everyone else seemed to know what was happening. He sat there until about 9 p.m., when the AP came around the counter and said: "Well, you can go now". He told him where to catch a public bus to downtown Roswell, and Bob called Bobbie from a pay phone he found in the hallway.

She shared the sad news with him that John F. Kennedy was dead. Was he catching a bus home?

"Yeah, but I'm in Roswell."

"What? What are you doing in Roswell?"

Good question. "We'll talk about it when I get home."

The Greyhound bus left at 11:00 p.m. When it pulled into the first stop on its route, Bob got off and bought a candy bar and some crackers -- the first things he'd had to eat since that last bite of breakfast more than 17 hours earlier. They pulled into Colorado Springs between 8:00 and 8:45 the next morning, and Bobbie was at the station to meet him. On the drive home he told her the story of his flight. Both felt it was merely a hitch in a terrible day. His plane was probably diverted as a part of the alert. And yet, both agreed not to discuss it with others.

They couldn't define it, but both had a feeling that he'd stepped into danger. He would later tell his brother about the flight, when Paul and his wife drove up to visit them from Leesville, Louisiana. But, that weekend -- like the rest of America -- Bob and Bobbie watched the national tragedy on television -- with one big difference.

Late Saturday, November 23rd, Bob hunched forward on the couch, stared intently at the TV, shook his head and looked again.

"That guy," he said to Bobbie. "That guy looks just like the little guy who was on the airplane."

"Are you nuts?" she said. "It couldn't be him. He's in jail."

"I swear, that's the little guy who got on the plane."

"Well," Bobbie said, "keep quiet about it."

One day later, the little guy -- Lee Harvey Oswald -- was dead.

# Chapter 5

# Enter the CIA

Bobbie was weeding the flowers in the front yard. It was a beautiful May day in 1964 -- six months after the flight she and her husband had decided not to mention -- and things were going well. Bob had received his promotion the first of the year, just a couple of weeks after the Johnson administration had totally reversed Kennedy's Vietnam policy. December 6, 1963, Secretary of State Dean Rusk had cabled Vietnam ambassador Henry Cabot Lodge that "The President has expressed his deep concern that our effort in Vietnam be stepped up to highest pitch." [10] And on December 19 and 20, Lodge told Vietnam leaders the US would be in that country to help "as long as help was needed." [11]

One week after the assassination, Johnson had asked Chief Justice Warren to chair a commission that would look into the assassination. Warren had declined, but later that day Johnson had summoned him to the White House. Rumors were circulating about conspiracies, he told Warren. The rumors had to be squelched, the nation had to be calmed, and only he had the reputation for integrity that could ensure domestic and international tranquility. He had to do it, Johnson said.[12]

Warren reluctantly accepted and the Warren Commission was underway, its duty, according to its Chief Counsel H. Lee Rankin: "to reassure this country and the world not only that we can protect our President but that accused criminals can be treated fairly."[13] This coming from a committee that was investigating how a president and his alleged assassin were both murdered in broad daylight before scores of witnesses.

But things got stranger, as Rankin explained that this "reassurance" would be accomplished through investigation of six major areas:

1. Oswald's activities on November 22.
2. Oswald's background.
3. Oswald's career.
4. Oswald's murder.
5. Ruby's background.
6. Procedures to protect President Kennedy.

As Mark Lane pointed out in his landmark book, *Rush to Judgement*, this key commission overlooked one key area -- "Who Killed the President?" But, it had already been decided well before the commission was even formed that Lee Harvey Oswald was the lone assassin.

Oswald was named and identified as the lone assassin while newly sworn in President Lyndon Johnson was flying back to Washington with Kennedy's corpse. The word came from McGeorge Bundy, the President's Assistant for National Security Affairs. Bundy had been at the Pentagon when the president was shot. He spent the rest of the afternoon in the White House Situation Room in telephone conversation with Johnson on Air Force One. His message -- Oswald was the killer, and he had acted alone. This was before Oswald was charged with anything.[14]

In addition, November 24th, two days after the assassination, FBI Director J. Edgar Hoover told Johnson in a phone conversation: "The thing that I am most concerned about...is having something issued so we can convince the public that Oswald is the real assassin." The FBI's report, concluding that Oswald acted alone was transmitted to Johnson December 9th, a little more than a week after the Warren Commission was created. [15]

Bob Vinson was happy in his administrative work at Ent Air Force Base, and both he and Bobbie were happy in their Colorado Springs home, planning to retire there when Bob had served his 20 years.

But that day in May, as Bobbie worked in the yard, a neighbor -- a Major Grable -- walked over and asked: "Bobbie, what have you and Bob been doing?"

"Nothing much," she smiled.

"Well, you must have been doing something because there've been an awful lot of people out here going all over the neighborhood asking questions about you two, wanting to know what kind of people you are, what you talk about, all of that kind of thing."

"What?"

"Yeah, they're all over the place asking about you two."

A chill ran up Bobbie's spine to know people were asking her neighbors all about Bob and her right under their noses, and -- when Bob asked at the base -- no one knew who or why. Then, October 15, 1964, Captain Robert E. Cole gave Bob a large envelope filled with papers to fill out. They included a Personal History Statement (DD

*Flight from Dallas*

Form 398) and a Secrecy Agreement -- one set for him and one for Bobbie.

"I already had the highest security clearance -- a crypto clearance -- to work at NORAD (North American Air Defense Command), so I assumed it was an update of some kind," he says. "You know, usually in the military, you don't ask, you just go ahead and do it. But Bobbie didn't like it".

Bobbie didn't see why an airman's wife should be required to fill out and sign a personal history statement, let alone a secrecy agreement. She had never had to sign anything like this before, and she knew of no other Air Force wife who had. She said she wouldn't do it. But when Bob told Captain Cole, the captain was insistent.

"It doesn't mean anything," he said. "It's just something they have to have. But they have to have them both".

Finally, Bobbie filled out and signed the papers. And then, in November, a set of top-secret orders came through Captain Cole. Bob was to fly to Washington D.C. and call a phone number. Purpose of the trip was listed as "For interview at HQUSAF in conjunction with a Special Project." None of Bob's superior officers claimed to know anything about the strange orders.

He was to leave Wednesday, November 20 on the shuttle from Ent to Andrews Air Force Base, and was scheduled to return December 9.

So on November 20 Bob flew into Andrews and called the number on the order. A man answered and told him to report to the first barracks after he entered the gate at nearby Fort Myer Army Base in Virginia. Bob took the bus to Fort Myer, and at that barracks, a guard told him to take a room and relax.

"A bus will be here at 8:00 Monday morning," he said. "Get on it."

Bob settled in, called Bobbie, and got something to eat at a little cafe in the PX. When he got back to the barracks, he received a long distance call from his brother-in-law, Ray Hall, in Lockhart, telling him his dad was very ill. Bob thought about bolting and going to Alabama to be with his father. Instead, he told Ray to keep him posted. If his father's condition worsened, he'd go.

And so he spent a nerve-wracking weekend worrying about his dad (who eventually recovered), hanging around the barracks in case his brother-in-law called, and wondering all the while why he'd been so mysteriously summoned.

Monday morning, the bus arrived, and he climbed aboard, joining about a dozen Air Force, Army and Navy personnel and civilians, all of whom -- like him -- kept quiet for the drive to Langley, Virginia, and up the drive with the "Restricted Area," "Keep Out" signs. Then someone said; "Hey, this is the CIA."

Completed in 1960, the CIA complex was a giant modern structure on a wooded 125-acre tract eights miles from downtown Washington.[16] The bus unloaded at the main building, and the group was taken to a room on the second floor. There, Bob was separated from the group, and taken to a room where he joined a different group of 15 to 20 men in four hours of written psychological testing.

They lunched in the cafeteria, then spent three hours undergoing rigorous physical examinations. Each was told not to speak to anyone of anything they heard or saw and at the end of the day, each signed a Secrecy Agreement dated December 1, 1964, in which each pledged never to divulge anything related to his recruitment by the CIA at the risk of government reprisal.

At 4 p.m., he was directed to the bus, where he rejoined the original group and -- again in silence -- they rode back to the Fort Myer, where he again spent the night.

Tuesday was the same routine -- psychological tests in the morning, physical examinations the afternoon, then back to Fort Myer. Wednesday brought a two-hour lie detector test, followed by more psychological tests in the morning, and more physical exams in the afternoon. Thursday was the same.

Friday, after more psychological tests, the group had lunch and sat drinking coffee as one by one, they were called from the room and ushered into a large conference room. Bob's turn was at about 1 p.m., and he strained his eyes to see his hosts, eight to 10 civilians sitting at a large U-shaped table in semi-darkness, while a spotlight struck him in the eyes as he sat at one end of the U.

They didn't introduce themselves, didn't even say they were with the CIA. Instead one of them told him they wanted him to "come to work for us."

"I don't want to do that," Bob said.

"Why not?"

"Well, I'm going to be discharged in a couple of years and my wife and I want to retire in Colorado Springs. I've already got a retirement job lined up there."

"We'll make it worth your while."

"I've already built our retirement house there."

"We can take care of that. You'll be compensated for it."

"But I just don't care to go wherever it is you want me to go. I'm happy where I am."

"But we'll make it worth your while."

"I just don't want to go."

The discussion droned on, the civilians taking turns asking questions and responding to his answers from out of the darkness. No one ever said a word about the nature of his duties in this new employment, or about anything in his background, including his 1963 flight in and out of Dallas. They just kept telling him he should "go with us."

Finally, there was silence. Then someone said: "OK. Well, you know where to go to get the plane back to Colorado Springs, don't you?"

"Yes, I think I do."

"Go outside and catch the bus and it'll take you to another bus you can ride to the airport."

And that was it. Just like that, four days of the most intense testing Bob had ever endured were over, as was the strangest job interview he'd ever encountered. The same bus with the same guys on it took him to Fort Myer, where another bus took him and the others to

*Flight from Dallas*

Baltimore-Washington Airport, and a few hours later, he was home telling the crazy story to Bobbie.

"You think this has anything to do with the flight from Washington to Roswell?" he asked her finally, giving voice to the thought both of them had been harboring.

"If it does," she replied, "don't say anything about it because a lot of the those people have been eliminated."

They both knew what Bobbie meant by "those people" -- people who, by accident or design, had special knowledge about the assassination, and over the past year had died in mysterious, violent ways. During the period of the Warren Commission investigation alone, a minimum of 21 potential witnesses suffered violent deaths. Another 16 would die violent deaths during investigations by later committees.[17]

The thought made Bob angry, but it also made him cautious. Only 18 months to go, and he'd be out of all this. He'd just serve out his time.

But that's not how it worked.

In February, 1965. His superiors called him in and said: "We're sorry to lose you, Bob, but these orders came down from headquarters, and we can't do anything about them." The orders transferred him from Ent Air Force Base to the 1129th USAF Activity Squadron at Boling Air Force Base, Washington D.C. But along with the order came instructions to report *not* to Washington but to Detachment One, 1129th Air Special Activities Squadron in Las

Vegas, Nevada. And, once again, he was to go to there and dial a phone number for further orders.

"There's too much to do. We've got to sell our house," Bob said. "We've got to pack and find a place and..."

"We've already got orders to move you," an officer said. "We'll do all the packing and take care of everything. Just put the house up for sale."

"But..." He had a hundred reasons for not going. But none mattered. That was that.

He and Bobbie decided they'd try to sell the house on their own without going through a realtor. The house at 1938 Wynkoop was their baby, their pride and joy, built to their specifications. They'd never get what they had in it, but orders were orders.

Bob put an ad in the *Colorado Springs Gazette.*

The morning the ad ran, a couple called and asked if they could see the house. They looked at it, said, "We'll take it. We'll meet you at First National Bank and sign all the documents." They paid the asking price with no haggles, no requests.

There was no doubt in Bob's mind who had really bought the house or for whom he would be working. This despite the fact that he'd told them over and over again that he didn't want to work for them. And why was it so important to them that they employ a guy who had only 18 more months before retirement? He told Bobbie it would be all right. Just 18 months. It would be all right.

But he told himself to be very careful and quiet.

*Flight from Dallas*

Robert G. Vinson today.

Seventeen year old soldier Bob Vinson.

*Flight from Dallas*

Vinson with class in Okinawa at the school he and his squadron adopted.

*James P. Johnston & Jon Roe*

Bob and Bobbie Vinson in the 1960's.

Carl Vinson, relative of Robert G. Vinson and Chairman of the House Armed Services Committee. The longest serving member of Congress until 1994. Presidential Medal of Freedom with Special Distinction.

Fred Vinson, a relative of Robert G. Vinson, served a total of six terms in the U.S. House of Representatives. He also served on the U.S. Court of Appeals and as Treasury Secretary prior to being named Chief Justice of the Supreme Court by President Truman in 1946.

*Flight from Dallas*

HEADQUARTERS
**NORTH AMERICAN AIR DEFENSE COMMAND**
ENT AIR FORCE BASE, COLORADO, 80912

AREA CODE 303
635-8911
EXT: 2108

IN REPLY REFER
TO: NEEC

FEB 14 1963

SUBJECT: NCO of the Month

THRU: Deputy Chief of Staff, Communications and Electronics
Hq North American Air Defense Command
Ent Air Force Base, Colorado

TO: Commander
4608th Support Squadron
Ent Air Force Base, Colorado

    1. In compliance with your letter, subject as above, dated 2 Aug 63, it is recommended that SSgt R. G. Vinson, AF14145079, be named NCO of the Month for the 4608th Support Squadron.

    2. Sergeant Vinson, in his assignment as Chief Clerk, Directorate of Electronics, Deputy Chief of Staff for Communications and Electronics, has demonstrated outstanding efficiency in all his duties. For example, the filing system he has arranged for the directorate has been examined by other Chief Clerks within NORAD and, in many instances, they have indicated that they would try to adopt this system for their office. He is a willing worker and does not hesitate to accept any responsibility offered him and neither does he hesitate to accept additional responsibilities when the need arises. Sergeant Vinson is quiet and unassuming in his work, personable, and diplomatic. He is well thought of by all his associates and maintains excellent working relationships with his co-workers and superiors.

    3. At the present time Sergeant Vinson is continuing to pursue an off-duty education program toward a degree in Business Law and Accounting. Since his assignment to Ent Air Force Base he has completed, either through class work or GED tests, an equivalent of more than two years' college level work. At the present time he is enrolled in two off-duty courses with the University of Colorado Extension Center and is preparing himself for the GED college level tests.

Vinson receives NCO of the Month at NORAD.

4. Sergeant Vinson is active outside of the military. He is a member of the Ent Chapter of the Toastmasters International and of the newly-formed Methodist Church Social Club affiliated with Saint Paul's Methodist Church.

J. K. PREWITT
Colonel, USAF
Director of Electronics

NELC     1st Ind     635-8911 Ext 2228

Hq North American Air Defense Command, Ent Air Force Base, Colorado    FEB 14 1963

TO: Commander, 4608th Support Squadron, Ent Air Force Base, Colorado

I am aware of Sergeant Vinson's performance of duty, and highly recommend him for this award.

W. B. LATTA
Brig Gen, USA
DCS/Comm and Elect

Vinson receives NCO of the Month at NORAD

*Flight from Dallas*

Vinson receives the Joint Service Commendation Medal

Vinson receives his sergeant's stripes.

*Flight from Dallas*

**RESTRICTED**

## FLIGHT CHARACTERISTICS

The C-54 has smooth, easy, and effective controllability at all speeds from a stall to 200 mph IAS. At speeds greater than 200 mph the elevators and rudder controls become increasingly stiff as the speed increases. This is a safety factor to prevent sudden maneuvers at high speeds, which might place excessive strains on the structure.

Because of this stiffness of the controls at high speeds, it is better to use the elevator trim tab, instead of the control column, to bring the nose up. With the trim tab you get a smoother and more positive action, without the danger of overcontrolling. Move the tab gently, however, because in spite of its definite positive action, you don't get the feel from it which you get from the control column.

The airplane has no dangerous or unexpected stall characteristics.

### Restricted Maneuvers

The C-54 is restricted to normal level flight. Regardless of what you have been flying, remember that the Skymaster is a transport, and hasn't the remotest resemblance to a fighter, in appearance or operation. The airplane has safety factors built into it which make it one of the safest ships the Army operates. You lose those safety factors when you ignore the limitations placed on its operation, and then you get into trouble.

Do not exceed the speeds given in the following airspeed limitations table:

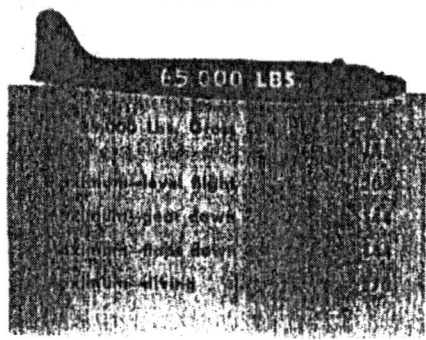

104                                    RESTRICTED

A Douglas C-54, the type of airplane that made the flight to and out of Dallas.

Map locating where the plane landed in Dallas.

*Flight from Dallas*

Aerial photo of the landing site taken January 4, 1964.

*James P. Johnston & Jon Roe*

| REQUEST AND AUTHORIZATION — TEMPORARY DUTY TRAVEL OF MILITARY PERSONNEL (If more space is required, continue on reverse, identifying items by number.) | DATE 25 Nov 64 |
|---|---|

**REQUEST FOR AUTHORIZATION**

4600 AB WG (WOCAS) Ent AFB, Colo 80912
*issuing authority*
4600 AB WG (CBPO-1asgmt) Ent AFB, Colo 80912

2. TYPE NAME, GRADE AND TITLE OF AUTHORIZED OFFICIAL: FREDERICK J SODOMKA CAPT USAF, Consolidated Base Personnel
3. SIGNATURE OF AUTHORIZED OFFICIAL
4. PHONE NR. 2385

1. REQUEST TDY BE AUTHORIZED AS INDICATED IN ITEMS 5 THROUGH 12.

**TEMPORARY DUTY TRAVEL ORDERS**

5. THE FOLLOWING INDIVIDUAL(S) WILL PROCEED AS INDICATED, UPON COMPLETION WILL RETURN TO PROPER STATION.

| GRADE | NAME (First name, middle initial, last name, AFSN) | ORGANIZATION | SECURITY CLEARANCE FOR PERIOD OF TDY |
|---|---|---|---|
| SSGT | R. G. VINSON, AF14145079 CAFSC 70250 | Det #1, 4608 Spt Sq | SECRET |

6. DEPART ON OR ABOUT 29 Nov 64
7. APPROXIMATE NR. OF DAYS (include travel time) 6
8. DOAV

9. SPECIFIC PURPOSE OF TDY: For interview at Hq USAF in conjunction with a Special Project.

10. ITINERARY: VARIATIONS IN ITINERARY AUTHORIZED
FROM: Ent AFB, Colo
TO: Arlington 8, Virginia
RETURN TO: Ent AFB, Colo

11. SPECIAL INSTRUCTIONS: ...rival in the Washington DC area, airman will report by telephone... will report to the 1120 Spt Gp, Ft Myer, South Area, Arlington... between the hours 0830 and 1200, 1 Dec 64. It is imperative that airman report on date... during hours specified above. 2 cys of this order and a cy of any paid voucher will be forwarded to Hq Comd USAF (CAF), Bolling AFB, 25,...

12. MODES OF TRAVEL. A. ☐ TRAVEL BY _____ DIRECTED WHEN AVAILABLE. B. ☐ TPA... TIME BY COMMON CARRIER (rail or bus) IS _____ DAYS. TRAVEL TIME IN EXCESS IS CHARGEABLE TO DELAY ENROUTE AUTHORIZED IN ITEM 8. C. ☐ TPA. THIS MODE OF TRANSPORTATION HAS BEEN DETERMINED TO BE MORE ADVANTAGEOUS TO THE GOVERNMENT. D. ☒ OTHER. Commercial or military air, bus or rail authorized.

**AUTHORIZATION**

13. AUTHORITY AFM 39-11 & Ltr DAF (AFPMPFC) 3190-F8, 17 Nov 64, TDY of Amn
14. DATE 25 November 1964
15. SPECIAL ORDER NR. T-857

16. DESIGNATION AND LOCATION OF APPROVING HEADQUARTERS: HEADQUARTERS 4600 AB WING (ADC), UNITED STATES AIR FORCE, ENT AIR FORCE BASE COLORADO

17. APPROPRIATION ACCOUNTING SYMBOL: 5753400 3056116 P458 2113 2133 2593 S503700

19. REQUEST FOR TDY IS APPROVED AND WILL BE PERFORMED. TDN.
FOR THE COMMANDER

DISTRIBUTION (if required)
1 - Indiv
2 - 1120 Spt Gp Ft Myer, Arlington Va
2 - USAF (AFPMPFC1)
2 - Hq Comd, USAF (CAF) Bolling AFB DC
  - 1ASGMTS AR ER/FR DR&A I&OP
  - CF-T (Mrs Frock)

20. SIGNATURE ELEMENT OF ORDERS ISSUING OFFICIAL
BLAKE A SMITH
Major, USAF
Chief Admin Sv

AF FORM 626  PREVIOUS EDITIONS OF THIS FORM MAY BE USED.

*Flight from Dallas*

Item 11 (Cont'd) Military air is directed upon departure from this st.... Airman will report to Passenger Service Section, Bas Operations, Bldg..., not later than 0700 hours, 29 Nov 64 for scheduled departure at 0800 hou.., 29 Nov 64. If TDY is terminated prior to return flight, airman will re... to MATS Passenger Service Counter, Andrews AFB, Washington, DC for purp... of cancellation of return flight. ETD of return flight 0800 hours, 9 ...

Vinson's orders to report to Arlington, VA.

| PERMANENT CHANGE OF STATION ORDER — MILITARY | | 1. INDIVIDUAL WP ON PCS AS SHOWN BELOW |
|---|---|---|
| 2. GRADE, LAST NAME, FIRST, MIDDLE INITIAL, AFSN<br>TSGT VINSON, R. G., AF14145079 | 3. SHIPPING APSC (Officer) | 4. CAFSC (Airman) 70270 | 5. □ OVER 4 YEARS SERVICE (AIC Only) |
| 6. UNIT, MAJOR AIR COMMAND AND ADDRESS OF UNIT FROM WHICH RELIEVED<br>4608 Spt Sq (ADC)<br>Ent AFB, Colo 80912 & with dy Det #1, NORAD | 7. UNIT MAJOR AIR COMMAND AND ADDRESS OF UNIT TO WHICH ASSIGNED AND DUTY STATION IF APPROPRIATE<br>1129 USAF Sp Actys Sq (Hq Comd)<br>P.O. Box 8C, Bolling AFB, D.C. 20332 & with dy Det 1, 1129 USAF Sp Actys Sq, Las Vegas, Nevada | 8. PURPOSE OF REASSIGNMENT IF OTHER THAN DUTY |
| 9. REPORT TO COMDR, NEW ASSIGNMENT NLT<br>17 May 65 | 10. REPORT AT NEW ASSIGNMENT NLT ___ DAYS AFTER DEPARTURE FROM CONUS PORT OF ENTRY UNIT | 11. DAVP Yes | 12. EDCSA 23 Apr 65 |

Vinson's orders to report to Las Vegas.

*Flight from Dallas*

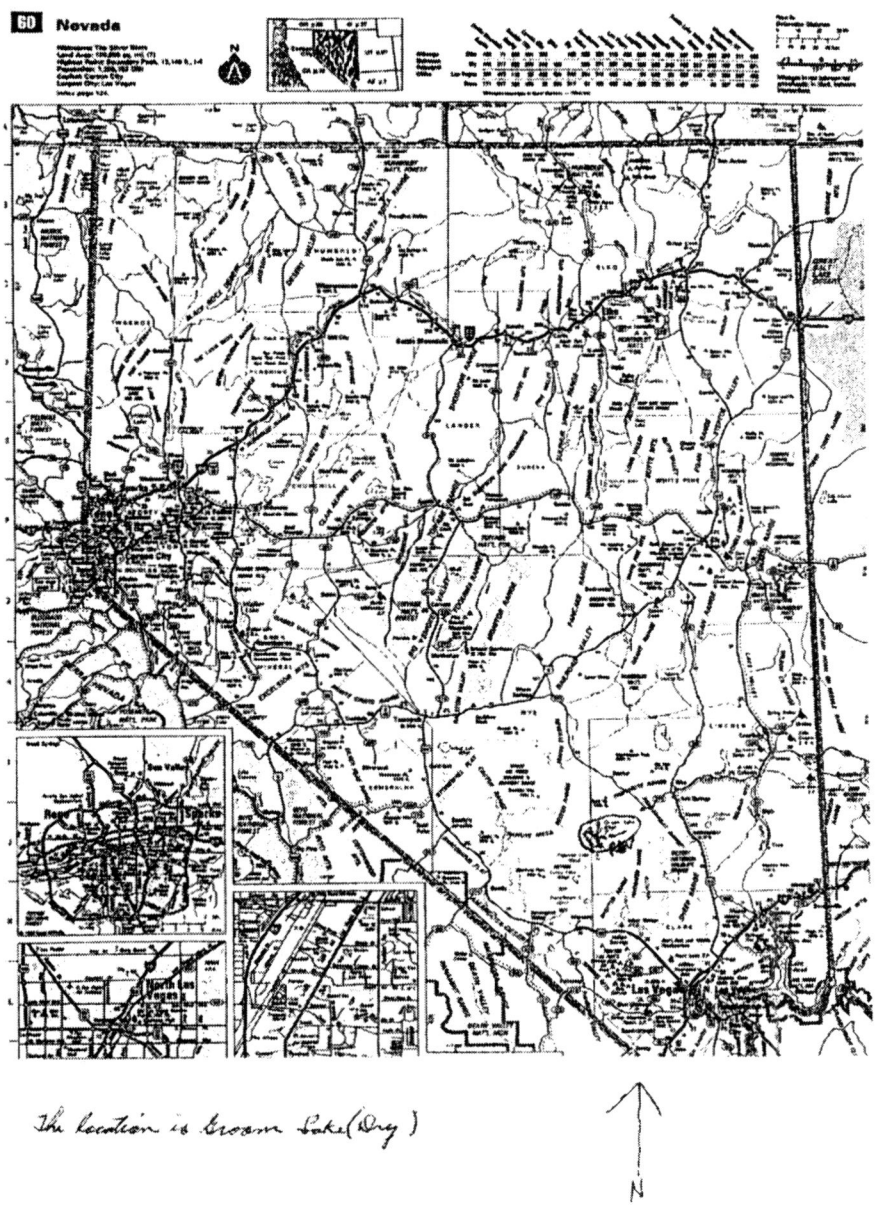

The location is Groom Lake (Dry)

Map depicting Site 51 where Vinson was stationed by CIA.

*Vinson's Retirement Order*

*Flight from Dallas*

**SMALL BUSINESS ADMINISTRATION**
120 SOUTH MARKET STREET
WICHITA, KANSAS 67202

June 26, 1974

Robert G. Vinson
3329 West 16th St. North
Wichita, KS  67203

Dear Mr. Vinson:

During recent months you have worked closely with and have thoughtfully counseled one of the many small businesses so vital to the nation's welfare. This service will contribute much to the successful operation of these firms, which is the primary objective of Small Business Administration's Small Business Institute Counseling Program.

Your efforts in advising on accounting, credit, finance, advertising, marketing, personnel, sales, inventory, and other such difficult day-to-day business problems have been extremely helpful. Businessmen often have to cope unaided with all such problem areas, so they have certainly valued your contributions.

Please accept our Business Counseling Certificate officially recognizing completion of your assigned project in our Small Business Institute Counseling Program. This program has served exceedingly well as a way to bring university expertise and "know-how" to firms anxious to have such help. Further, the Small Business Administration believes you have substantially broadened your own insight into the practicalities of small business challenges.

Congratulations and sincere thanks,

Clayton Hunter, Acting District Director

**Vinson receives Small Business Administration Counseling Certificate.**

*James P. Johnston & Jon Roe*

**WOLF TECHNICAL SERVICES, INC.**
Technical Investigations
Forensic Analysis
Engineering Consultants

6836 Hawthorn Park Drive • Indianapolis, IN 46220-3909 • (317) 842-6075 • FAX (317) 842-6974
Illinois (773) 881-8826 • Ohio (937) 548-0500 • Wisconsin (414) 646-9331

## James S. Sobek, P.E.

**AREAS OF SPECIALIZATION:**

Expert analysis of automotive collisions, railroad grade crossing collisions, and incidents involving physics and mechanics of motion. Strong emphasis on human vision, lines-of sight, lighting, visibility under the influence of glare, darkness, fog, etc., stereoscopic depth perception and other vision issues. Developer of analytical tools to determine illumination and visibility under locomotive headlamps. Extensive (40 years) experience in analog electronic systems including audio sound recording, signal processing systems, high fidelity and stereo playback equipment. Strong computer programming skills.

**EDUCATION:**

**Wellsville High School, Wellsville, NY**
1960 Duane H. Anderson Science Medal recipient

**U.S. Navy: Honorable Discharge, FTM-2 (Missiles)**
Fire Control Technician "A" School
Weapons Designation System - 7 "C" School
Weapons Designation System - 9 "C" School
USAFI Physics Course
Electronics Refresher School
Cold Weather Survival School
AN/SPG-55A "C" School (Terrier Beamrider missile)
AN/SPG-55B "C" School (Terrier Semi-active homing missile)

**Thiel College, Greenville, PA**
Bachelor of Arts Degree - June 1968
    Major: Physics   Minors: Math/Chemistry
    Languages: French & Russian
    Overall GPA: 9.12 (Dean's List)
Advanced Level Courses
    Classical Lens Design - UCLA (Kingslake)
    Engineering Uses of Aerial Photography - IUPUI (Dr. Robert Miles)
    Tribology (Wear and Lubrication) - IUPUI
    FORTRAN - Naval Avionics Center
    VAX 11/70 Operating System - Digital Equipment Corp.
    Spread Spectrum Systems
    Global Positioning System and Navigation Systems
    Federal Railroad Administration Track Safety Standards

*Serving Our Clients For Over 20 Years*

James S. Sobek
Page Two

**WORK EXPERIENCE:**

JAN 1995 to Present:
Wolf Technical Services, Inc., Indianapolis, IN
SENIOR ACCIDENT ANALYST: Specializing in automotive accident reconstruction with emphasis on analysis of lighting, optics, visibility/conspicuity, aerial photography, photogrammetry, and image processing. Particularly heavily involved in analysis of railroad grade crossing collisions. Analysis of the physics issues of exterior ballistics, ladder dynamics, friction, and other questions involving mechanical dynamics. Electronic signal analysis, particularly analog sound recordings.

OCT 1993 to JAN 1995:
Wolf Technical Services, Inc., Indianapolis, IN
TECHNICAL DIRECTOR: Responsible for the day-to-day operations of the company. Review and approval of forensics engineering work.

APR 1988 to OCT 1993:
Wolf Technical Services, Inc., Indianapolis, IN
SENIOR ACCIDENT ANALYST: Specialized in automotive accident reconstruction with emphasis on analysis of lighting, optics, visibility, aerial photography, photogrammetry, and image processing. Particularly heavily involved in analysis of railroad grade crossing collisions. Analysis of the physics issues of exterior ballistics, ladder dynamics, friction, etc. Broad scientific involvement.

JUN 1987 to APR 1988:
Naval Avionics Center, Indianapolis, IN
DSMAC PROGRAM MANAGER, D/906.2 (Electrical Engineer): Responsible for the production of Digital Scene Matching Area Correlator (DSMAC), the autonomous precision electro-optical missile guidance system currently used on the Navy's TOMAHAWK cruise missile. Also responsible for the design and development of the DSMAC IIA follow-on system.

DEC 1986 to JUN 1987:
Naval Avionics Center, Indianapolis, IN
ASSISTANT TO THE EXECUTIVE DIRECTOR, D/004.
Senior Management grooming position

JUN 1986 to DEC 1986:
Naval Avionics Center, Indianapolis, IN
GLOBAL POSITIONING SYSTEM PROG MGR, D/909:
Responsible for all GPS systems integration activities at the Center. Developed GPS equipment second-sources for the Joint Program Office.

OCT 1984 to JUN 1986:
Naval Avionics Center, Indianapolis, IN
DEPUTY PROG. MGR. NAV/INSTRUM/DISPLAYS, D/072.71:
Responsible for development, production, and maintenance of aircraft navigation and display components.

James S. Sobek
Page Three

| | |
|---|---|
| MAR 1983 to OCT 1984: | **Naval Avionics Center, Indianapolis, IN**<br>BRANCH MANAGER, D/925 (Electrical Engineer): Responsible for design, development, production and maintenance of system components of the Navy's television-guided Walleye missile system. Missile system trajectory and response to guidance inputs from pilots were important components of my work. |
| JUN 1968 to MAR 1983: | **Naval Avionics Center, Indianapolis, IN**<br>RESEARCH PHYSICIST, B/824 (Physicist) Co-inventor (see Patents section below) of the Digital Scene Matching Area Correlator system, the precision electro-optical guidance system used on the Navy's TOMAHAWK cruise missile. Jointly responsible for the system engineering aspects of the DSMAC. Solely responsible for the system's electro-optical design and the image processing techniques used in preparing the reference imagery. This work required the consideration of missile flight dynamics and the airframe's ability to respond to guidance inputs. Ballistic trajectory computations were a strong component of the work. Additional work creating a digital link simulator for early TOMAHAWK guidance development. Developed a technique for using an early video tape recorder to record Ships Inertial Navigation System data directly from data ports. |
| Mid-1979 to Present: | **Integral Software, Indianapolis, IN**<br>Owner/operator of software programming service, consulting, training and writing custom software for various applications. |
| Summers and Vacations, 1964 to 1967: | **Robert Lewis, General Contractor, Alfred, NY**<br>Assistant in all phases of general contracting work. Was offered a permanent position as partner. |

**COMPUTER SYSTEMS:**

Proficient in MS-DOS based systems: particularly TKSolver, BASIC, WINDOWS 95, and the Internet via AOL.

**PUBLICATIONS:**

*Digital Scene Matching Area Correlator* by Jon R. Carr and James S. Sobek (SPIE Proceedings, July 1980, San Diego)

Numerous classified papers and presentations with the U.S. Navy on aerial imaging, image processing and photogrammetry.

*Three-Dimensional Computerized Photogrammetry and Its Application to Accident Reconstruction* by M.D. Pepe, J.S. Sobek, and G.J. Huett. (SAE 890739, March 1989)

*The Accuracy of Three-Dimensional Computerized Photogrammetry as Demonstrated by Field Tests* by J.S. Sobek, M.D. Pepe and D.A. Zimmerman (SAE 930662, March 1993)

James S. Sobek
Page Four

**LICENSES:**

Registered Professional Engineer, Indiana License Number: PE60890004

**MEMBERSHIPS:**

Cruise Missiles Association
Indiana Transportation Museum
Optical Society of America
Society of Automotive Engineers

**PATENTS:**

Digital Scene Matching Area Correlator
(secrecy order number 146,981; assigned to U.S. Navy)

Trucker's Log Chek®, U.S. Patent No. 5,142,486

Current as September 8, 1998

Curriculum Vitae of James S. Sobek, P.E.

*James P. Johnston & Jon Roe*

Central Intelligence Agency

Washington D.C. 20505

1 9 FEB 1998

James P. Johnston, Esquire
The Johnston Law Offices
800 N. Market
P.O. Box 3089
Wichita, Kansas  67201-3089

Reference:  P95-0806

Dear Mr. Johnston:

This is in response to your letter dated 4 May 1995 in which you appealed on behalf of your client, Mr. Robert Griel Vinson, our lack of response to your 18 January 1995 Freedom of Information Act and Privacy Act request on behalf of your client for information on himself.  Specifically, requested "...any and all documents created, obtained by or received by CIA at any time concerning [himself] including confidentiality agreements."

Your appeal has been presented to the appropriate members of the Agency Release Panel,            , Information Review Officer for the Directorate of Operations;          , Acting Information Review Officer for the Directorate of Administration; and          , Information Review Officer for the Directorate of Science and Technology.  Pursuant to the authority delegated under paragraphs 1900.51(a) and 1901.17(c) of Chapter XIX, Tittle 32 of the Code of Federal regulations (C.F.R.),           and            have directed that a thorough search be conducted of those records systems which we are required to search and which could reasonably be expected to contain documents responsive to your request.  Responsive material was located as a result of these searches.  A description of each document, the determinations made with respect to each, and the basis for each determination follow:

|   | Document Number and Description | Determination | Exemption Basis |
|---|---|---|---|
| 1. | Form DD398<br>20 October 1964 | Release in full | |
| 2. | Form 1066<br>3 December 1964 | Release in full | |
| 3. | Folder & record card 12 Jan 1964 | Release in part | (b)(3) |

*Flight from Dallas*

James P. Johnston, Esquire

    A copy of the documents as approved for release are enclosed. We appreciate your patience while your appeal was being considered.

                                Sincerely,

                                Chairman
                         Agency Release Panel

Enclosures

CIA Freedom of Information Act response proving Vinson's presence at CIA headquarters in Langley, VA.

*James P. Johnston & Jon Roe*

U.S. Department of Justice

Federal Bureau of Investigation

In Reply, Please Refer to
File No.

1801 North Lamar, Suite 300
Dallas, Texas 75202-1748
December 2, 1998

James P. Johnston
Johnston Law Offices, P.A.
800 N. Market
P.O. Box 3089
Wichita, Kansas 67201-3089

Dear Mr. Johnston:

    Please accept my apology for the delay in responding to your letters of September 21, 1998 and September 28, 1998, concerning information on the assassination of President John F. Kennedy. As you may already be aware, even though the assassination occurred over 35 years ago, our office continues to be inundated with inquiries regarding the events which transpired that infamous day in November 1963.

    We have reviewed your "abstract" of information relating to the experiences of your client, Robert G. Vinson. Mr. Vinson's recollections concern a series of events which transpired during a military flight he took following the shooting of President Kennedy. Mr. Vinson asserts that one of the passengers on the plane which traveled to Roswell Air Force Base in New Mexico resembled Lee Harvey Oswald. While we do not contest Mr. Vinson's observations, we must note that many individuals reported seeing "Oswald look-a-likes" during the period surrounding the assassination. Moreover, without specific information such as flight manifests, passenger lists and the like, it is unlikely that we would be able to ascertain the name of the passenger(s). While Mr. Vinson's recollections are interesting, there are no new allegations which would warrant further scrutiny by this office.

    Please note that in the interest of thoroughness and justice, the FBI has conducted numerous follow-up inquiries into new allegations regarding the assassination, and when appropriate, the results have been furnished to the Department of Justice.

    It is my understanding that presently there are over 350,000 pages of documents pertaining to the assassination currently available to be reviewed by the public at the National Archives in College Park, Maryland. Additionally, you should, under the Freedom Of Information Privacy Act (FOIPA), visit the National Archives and Records Administration on 7th and Pennsylvania, NW, Washington, D.C. (which houses record group 222, the Warren Commission Reports, and record group 233, the report from the House Select Committee on Assassinations); or the FBI FOIPA Reading Room at FBI Headquarters, Washington, D.C., to review these documents. If you desire to visit the FBI Reading Room, you must contact telephone number 202/324-8057 to make an appointment.

       Finally, the last resource which may be of assistance is the JFK Assassination Records Collection Act of 1992 (JFK ARCA) which mandates public disclosure and transfer of all related materials to the National Archives and Records Administration. You may want to contact the Board directly who are located in Washington, D.C. The Board is comprised of historians, Political Scientists, Archivists, and Lawyers. You may want to contact the Board directly to ascertain if there have been any recent releases of information concerning the topic of your inquiry. In the future, if I can be of any service to you, please feel free to contact our office as well as furnish any additional information that you deem appropriate.

Sincerely,

Danny A. Defenbaugh
Special Agent in Charge

By:

Wilbur M. Gregory, Jr.
Chief Division Counsel

RECEIVED
DEC 7 1998
Johnston Law Offices

FBI correspondence refusing investigation.

# Chapter 6

# Working for 'The Agency'

When an Air Force sergeant finally contacted Bob in Las Vegas, he wasted no time in confirming that the new employer was indeed the Central Intelligence Agency, and in telling Bob just how he and Bobbie would be living for the next 18 months. But that was four days after the Vinsons had arrived.

Their first day in town, a Thursday, Bob called the number from the Las Vegas motel at which he and Bobbie had stopped. There was no answer throughout the afternoon, but finally, that evening, someone answered and told him to move to another motel immediately. All expenses would be paid, and they were to wait for a phone call. They waited. Four days later, on Sunday night, an Air Force senior master sergeant who identified himself as Armentrout called to tell Bob he'd be stationed at a base near Mercury, 40 miles northwest of Las Vegas. He and Bobbie would rent a home in Las Vegas, and Bob would fly back and forth on weekends. He would, the NCO said, be working for the CIA.

But what would he be doing? He'd learn that when he got there.

He drove to the base Monday morning, getting a photo badge at the first gate, staffed by the Atomic Energy Commission, then exchanging badges at four more gates. He ended up at a small air base

*Flight from Dallas*

hidden from sight by mountains, nestled on the banks of dry Groom Lake. His job – administrative supervisor for base supply.

The area is now known to the public and to students of spying as Site 51, a base carved out of the desert in the middle of the Nellis Mountain Range, just north of the Atomic Energy Commission's Nevada Test Site. Its existence denied until recently by the U.S. Government, it was established in 1951 to test Douglas' new U2 spy plane. After that came the A-12, Blackbird SR 71, Stealth bomber B2, Stealth Fighter F-117 and most recently the Aurora.

In addition to those, reports are, and Bob confirms them, that stranger, more advanced experimental craft were tested there. That led to countless UFO sightings in the area, which became a mecca for UFO enthusiasts, just as happened in Roswell, New Mexico. [18]

Bob worked in the counter-intelligence operation, but he had reason to believe another operation – the experimental one – was going on at Roswell, N.M., and that those experimental craft were flown to Nevada for flight testing. "They were testing some of the most far-out things you could ever think of," Bob says today. "A lot of them were saucer shaped. And we did the testing. These were programs in their very early stages, and they had it pretty well blocked off so that they didn't have to fear others coming in and viewing them".

The UFO sightings were a standing joke at the base, where over lunch, they'd laugh about the strange stuff that went up the night before. Today, Bob says he believes people who say they saw flying saucers. But he doesn't believe those saucers came from outer space, even though the saucer madness is a great cover for the CIA. They're either from outer space or the witnesses are crazy. But they couldn't be manufactured right here by our own government, now could they?

Bob had breakfast there with Francis Gary Powers -- the U2 pilot shot down over the Soviet Union -- who came to work there as a consultant when he was repatriated to America.

Bob and Bobbie moved to 305 N. Gardenia Lane in Las Vegas. Each morning he would drive or take a standing shuttle from Las Vegas International Airport. He came back Friday, although now and then he'd catch the shuttle for a quick visit home Wednesday evening, and go back Thursday morning. Most often he'd drive up Monday, fly home Wednesday, fly back Thursday, and drive home Friday night.

A big part of Bob's job was to secure the materials to keep the SR-71, Blackbird spy plane flying. The spy planes carried no insignia. But one plane did -- a C-54 with the very same insignia on its tail Bob had noticed on the C-54 he climbed aboard at Andrews Air Force Base November 22, 1963. That's the same plane, he thought, and turned to ask Sgt. Armentrout to whom it belonged. They serviced Lockheed, Beech and some airlines that flew in and out of there.

"CIA," Armentrout said.

Recent reports are that today the base is closed and all experiments moved to sites in Utah and Colorado because of the growing radiation hazard and more space-oriented work.[19]

In the 18 months he worked there, no one said a word to Bob about the flight of November 22, 1963 and certainly he said nothing to anyone. If the CIA had forced him into their employment because of that day's flight, their plan was not to threaten or frighten him.

But he did -- along with others who worked there -- receive an extra cash payment each month from an officer who flew to Washington and brought back the money.

Perhaps, as far as the CIA was concerned, Robert Vinson was bought and paid for.

September 30, 1966, his orders show that Bob Vinson retired from Boling Air Force Base, Washington D.C., a base he'd never been near. He and Bobbie had looked forward to retirement before his assignment to Las Vegas. Now, they felt as if they'd been freed from a plush prison.

He'd been in the service 20 years, four months and 19 days and wore the World War II Victory medal, the Korean Service Medal, the United Nations Service Medal, the National Defense Service Medal, the Air Force Longevity Service Medal with Oakleaf Cluster, the Army and Air Force Joint Service Commendation Medal, the Air Force Outstanding Unit Award and the Pacific Air Force Achievement Certificate.

Over the past three years, they'd grown accustomed to looking beyond the obvious, questioning everything around them, looking for hidden meanings. Could they leave all this behind them now? What would the CIA consider to be the period of time covered by the secrecy agreements they had signed? What could the agency do if it decided Bob or Bobbie had broken their agreements. It wasn't fun living while looking over your shoulder.

They moved to Long Beach, California, where he had secured a job with an accounting firm. But three months later, Bobbie's brother called from Wichita, Kansas, with word that the firm doing accounting for his company was looking for help. Bob flew to Wichita that Thanksgiving of 1966 for an interview at Mobley, West, Jennings and Shaw, and went to work for them January 11, 1967.

In April, he landed a job with the City of Wichita, and worked his way up from administrative aide to Litter Control Director, supervising 64 employees and overseeing a $1.7 million budget.

Nineteen sixty seven was also the year New Orleans District Attorney Jim Garrison indicted and tried Clay Shaw for conspiracy to murder the president. The trial brought the first public showing of the famous Zapruder film of the shootings at Dealy Plaza. When Bob saw the film on television, he could see that President Kennedy was hit from at least two directions, not one, as the Warren Commission had concluded.

He and Bobbie talked about it, over and over again -- always alone, always troubled by what they knew and about who else might know it.

"It gnawed at him every day," Bobbie recalls today. "He wanted to share it. We both knew there was a good deal about that trip that wasn't right. But we were afraid if he got involved, they'd take away his retirement pay and maybe worse. We talked about the witnesses who had died under mysterious circumstances. We decided that -- since he'd signed that document that he wouldn't reveal anything he'd seen, we'd keep quiet." So he continued to carry the secret with him while hearing and reading new facts and theories.

It was in 1976 that Bob had asked an attorney for help in dealing with his secret. It was a lawyer in Wichita to whom Bob and Bobbie had turned for help in getting a defective car replaced by the manufacturer. Out of the blue, Bob told the lawyer the story of that flight from Dallas, and asked him what he should do about it?

It was a cry for help from a man who couldn't bear carrying such a secret. But the lawyer heard the tale in amazement, and then gave his advice -- "Don't tell a soul. For your own safety."

It was the same advice Bob and Bobbie had been giving each other. It made sense.

Except, more and more Bob knew, it was wrong.

He spoke to the attorney the year after the Select Committee on Intelligence of the House of Representatives declined to issue a report on its investigation of the assassination because President Gerald Ford would not certify that its findings would not harm national security.

But four years after that, in 1979, the House Select Committee on Assassinations concluded that Kennedy was probably the victim of a conspiracy, and that there was a "high probability" that at least two gunmen fired on him in Dallas.

Then in 1991 came Oliver Stone's movie, *JFK,* which suggested that agents from the FBI, CIA and the military conspired in the assassination.

And the nation indicated by polls and surveys that it continued to believe what most Americans had believed from the start -- that the Warren Report was incorrect, that there was a conspiracy.

In 1992, President George Bush signed Assassination Records Review Board legislation, providing that every government-held record relating to the assassination be made public at once, except for those that fell within enumerated exemptions, which would be released by 2017. However, the law states that the president can overrule such disclosure because "continued postponement is made necessary by an identifiable harm to the military, defense, intelligence operations, law enforcement, or conduct of foreign relations" and "the identifiable harm is of such gravity that it outweighs the public interest in disclosure."[20]

Maybe this was what Bob Vinson had been waiting for. A trustee of Riverlawn Christian Church in Wichita for 19 years, recipient of two awards from the Small Business Institute for counseling new businesses in Wichita, a regular and informed voter, he was as good a citizen as he knew how to be...except for that one duty he felt was his, but didn't know how to perform. And maybe this would let him do it.

He and Bobbie talked about the new legislation. Shouldn't this free them to talk about the flight? Couldn't he speak out now? They agreed that he should...if he could. A cautious man, who'd always followed orders, he felt he had to determine if his orders -- viewed in the light of this new legislation -- would allow him, at last, to share his story.

But who do you call, where do you turn? Who can you trust with such a question? As he watched the 10 o'clock television news one evening, the answer came to him. He had grown to trust one particular television news anchor. And he wasn't alone.

Most of southern Kansas trusted Larry Hatteburg. A prize-winning chief photographer who became an anchor at KAKE-TV, the ABC affiliate, Hatteberg in the year 2000, would be awarded a lifetime Emmy for a body of work, which was highlighted by his popular feature "Hatteberg's People" on the 10 o'clock newscast. Each report told the story of a person who -- though he or she seemed quite ordinary -- was actually extraordinary in some way or other, with an extraordinary story to tell. And Hatteberg's photography and narration were always sensitive and respectful. He struck Bob as a cautious sort who wouldn't get him in trouble.

One evening as they watched the news, Bob said to Bobbie: "I'm going to talk to Larry Hatteberg about the Kennedy assassination." She urged him to do so, and two days later he called Hatteberg and made an appointment. The two met, Hatteberg taped Bob's story and assured him he would check out not just Bob's reliability but what risks Bob would run by revealing his story.

A few days later, Bob got a phone call from Rep. Dan Glickman, congressman from Wichita's 4th Congressional District. Glickman (later Secretary of Agriculture) was then Chairman of the House Intelligence Oversight Committee.

Glickman said he'd talked with Hatteberg, and was calling to ask what questions or concerns Bob had. Bob told him about the secrecy agreement he had signed, and asked if his telling his story could cause problems. No, Glickman said. The intention of Congress in passing the Assassination Records Review Board Act was to get everything out in the open.

Hatteberg told Bob he'd checked him out with the anchorman's sources, and spent the next few days shooting background footage and editing the report, which aired as a three minute segment on KAKE-TV, Channel 10 at 10 p.m., November 23, 1993. Hatteberg began the segment by describing Bob as "not a man you would expect to have secrets, but..." Then, in interviews, newsreels and recreation, he told the story of that flight into and out of Dallas, and the CIA assignment that quickly followed. He said that Bob believed the job was connected with his being on the flight, and that the flight was connected to the assassination.

Why is Vinson coming forward with this information now, news anchor Mark Allen asked?

"Most of the information regarding the Kennedy Assassination has now been declassified, and so he felt it was alright to come forward," Hatteberg said. "And also, it's just something that he wanted to talk about, that he felt the public should know about. Just one piece of perhaps a very, very large puzzle."

"Maybe a larger piece than we know at this point," Allen said.

"Time will tell," Hatteberg replied.

The phone calls started that night. Most of them were from people who claimed they knew who really killed JFK, a surprising number of the suspects were in-laws. Bob listened politely, even to the cranks.

He had gotten his story out, but to what effect? Had telling his story done anyone any good? After years of paralyzing indecision, Bob might feel better inside, but the action itself didn't seem to have changed anything in the world around him.

Then came a phone call from James P. Johnston. That call would launch him on another journey no less mysterious, with no fewer twists and turns than he encountered on the flight from Dallas.

# Chapter 7

# Finding an Ally

Jim Johnston seems just the opposite of Bob Vinson. Rather than tending toward plump and quiet, he's thin and voluble. And no one's ever described him as mild-mannered.

Born in Wichita in 1929, he served in the Army in 1946-'47, then attended Wichita University on the GI Bill and then University of Kansas Law School. After serving as a hearing examiner for the Kansas Workers Compensation Commission, he went into private practice in Wichita..

He and his politically-active wife, Colleen, have six children and 16 grandchildren. One of their children and a granddaughter are attorneys in The Johnston Law Office P.A., where Colleen recently retired as business manager and Jim is still the very active senior member. It's an activist law office, representing working people against big business and big government. Office stationery bears the words: "Equal Justice for All." A volunteer trial attorney for the American Civil Liberties Union, he's also the publisher of "The Johnston Report," a no-holds-barred commentary on politics and social problems. He speaks before groups around the state on the Kennedy murder, which he believes was a conspiracy that reached into high levels of the federal government.

A small, vital man, he always lets you know where he stands -- proudly on the liberal side. He's the first to his feet after a speech, with a question that cuts through any generalities and obfuscations to the philosophical and social heart of the matter. He's always ready to argue a point, and he has more facts at his fingertips than most. Some consider him unnecessarily contentious, others see him as a gadfly who stimulates critical thought. But all agree he's a dedicated lawyer and an outspoken proponent for the little person.

In John F. Kennedy, he saw a patrician politician who (like Johnston's other political idol, Franklin D. Roosevelt) had just begun to take action on behalf of powerless Americans. Kennedy was pulling the United States back from support of expensive and dangerous extremist right wing causes around the world. He was breaking down racial and religious prejudice here at home and moving to bring a halt to the simmering cold war. Kennedy's speech at American University on June 10, 1963, on moderating the cold war was the first such speech by an American president. He was changing the course of politics in America, challenging the national security state which Johnston believed was drawing the U.S. toward a hot war with the Soviet Union.

And then he was killed.

Johnston doubted the Warren Commission's neat conclusions from the beginning, and his study of the work of many researchers before him led him to question everything the government said and did in regard to the case. He had talked and corresponded with experts and analysts throughout the United States and, with passage of the Assassination Materials Disclosure Act of 1992 (popularly referred to as the Assassination Records Review Act), had begun a modest search through the secret records of the government. Everything he read and learned from serious researchers led him to the need to learn more about what was then the most secret of US government agencies -- the CIA.

Jim's daughter, Casey Johnston Sloan, watched "Hatteberg's People" on Channel 10 the night of November 23, 1993. She promptly called her father to report on it, and Jim promptly called Hatteberg requesting a tape of the segment. What Bob Vinson said fit everything Johnston believed. He was convinced there was a second Oswald, an imposter, in Dallas to draw attention to the real Oswald, that there were shooters in front of, as well as behind, Kennedy's motorcade, and that the CIA was instrumental in it all. Here was an opportunity to request specific records from the CIA that would put Vinson at key places at key times.

Hatteberg gave him an air check of the piece, but wouldn't provide any of the out takes, and said any further information had to come from Bob Vinson. Johnston called Vinson at 3:05 the next afternoon and asked to meet with him.

Bob was cautious. He didn't know Jim Johnston, had no idea who he really represented. The strange phone calls he'd received had been jarring disappointments. He told Johnston that he and Bobbie had been having second thoughts about the wisdom of having contacted Hatteberg. But he'd think it over.

Jim left his business and home numbers, and asked that Vinson call him either way. He said he would.

Nothing.

December 8th, the anxious Johnston wrote the reticent Vinson asking for a meeting. "I do consider your experience to be valuable and possibly significant or I would not be bothering you about it."

December 10th, Bob called. Johnston was out of the office, and he left a message: "He doesn't want to give any interviews now. He is going out of town for the holidays and he might call you when he gets back."

Nothing.

February 15th, Jim sent a letter inviting Bob and Bobbie to lunch "for the purpose of getting acquainted with each other and not for an interview. I would simply like to explain to you the basis of my interest."

Well, Bob thought, the guy doesn't give up. What if he were just the person Bob had been hoping to interest in his story? But nothing as intimate as lunch. He met with Johnston at his office. He was impressed. Johnston asked for an in-depth interview about the flight of November 22, 1963, and he offered to represent Bob in getting documents related to it from the government. All free of charge.

But Bob still hesitated. Hatteberg was putting his story in a book, a collection of his reports, and -- even though he had no contract of any sort -- Bob didn't want to do anything that might interfere with or compromise that venture.

So went the discussion -- what discussion there was -- Johnston writing letters on May 19th and July 18th, urging in the second that "time is moving on for all of us and I earnestly believe that your full story should be made a matter of the printed record."

And on September 12, Jim wrote that he had called Hatteberg to insure that he had no problem with their talking. Hatteberg had none. "In fact," Jim wrote, "he voluntarily stated that he would call you and so advise you." But he also included in that letter a paragraph that jumped out at Bob and changed the way he viewed Johnston:

"Due to the fact that I still have not heard from you, I am beginning to assume that perhaps some representative of the U.S. government may have contacted you ... and possibly intimidated you about discussing your experience any further?? If this is the case, I would certainly voluntarily assist you in appropriate response if you desire."

It sounded as if Jim Johnston understood that one could fear government reprisal, that he didn't find it strange that Bob had hesitated all these years before speaking out. And the fact that he would volunteer to assist "in appropriate response" got Bob to thinking. Maybe he wasn't helpless against the CIA. Maybe a sincere lawyer who believed as he did could make a difference.

"I hadn't really known what to think," says Bob. "But after I got to know him, I knew that, like me, he was only trying to find out who killed Kennedy."

And so they came together -- opposites who had encountered years of frustration in their searches -- about to team up to find the truth.

The first thing Johnston did was record a full 52-page statement from Vinson and obtain copies of his official orders. In December of '94 Bob and Bobbie had retired to Florida, but correspondence and phone calls continued, and Bob returned in November 1996 to record an hour and 15 minute video tape of his story. Bob also offered to undergo a lie detector test if it ever became necessary.

On January 18, 1995, Johnston filed Freedom of Information Act (FOIA) requests for Bob's records with the Air Force and the CIA. He also requested from the Air Force any information about the flight from Andrews Air Force Base on that day.

The Air Force responded swiftly, saying it had no records of any such flight, because all flight logs were destroyed after one year. It also sent Bob's enlistment records, which contained nothing extraordinary.

The CIA was another matter.

Although it acknowledged receiving Johnston's request within 10 days (as required by law), the CIA provided nothing more until June 16, 1997 -- 28 months after the request. And then the response didn't come from the CIA, but the Air Force, which wrote that the CIA had asked it to release to Johnston some of Vinson's files that related to the agency. It enclosed his Air Force discharge, which took place at Nellis Air Force Base in Las Vegas.

Johnston was elated. The CIA had admitted it had files on Vinson and that he had worked at their base. It released nothing else until February 19, 1998 -- 37 months after the request -- and then very little. Thirteen records -- released only in part -- included CIA approval to recruit Bob, and a copy of his physical. So the CIA *admitted* that Bob had been ordered to its headquarters.

But one record dated December 3, 1964 (while Bob was being tested at CIA headquarters) was *denied* in full.

How could that document endanger national security? That was the reason the CIA gave for refusing to release it.

Only two items were released in full, both from 1964 -- the personal history form he had reluctantly filled out in Colorado Springs and the secrecy agreement he'd signed at CIA headquarters.

Bob was much relieved to see the secrecy agreement again. This was the piece of paper that hung over his head like a sword for 34 years. What was its power? Did the CIA have a record of enforcing such agreements? What could it do to Bob and Bobbie?

In person, it wasn't as intimidating as it had been in Bob's memory. It appeared that it related entirely to his recruitment and interviews, and could not be interpreted to apply to that plane ride of 1963. Besides, Johnston's research turned up the same basic conclusions reached by Victor Marchetti and John D. Marks in their 1974 book, *The CIA and the Cult of Intelligence*, in which they wrote that:

*All employees of the CIA are required to sign an agreement in which they promise not to reveal any information learned during their employment....The standard form of the agreement includes threats of prosecution and promises to deliver the most awful consequences upon the slightest violation. The only trouble with the threats is that until now they have been unenforceable. Apart from disclosure of information classified by the Atomic Energy Commission, it is not a crime to disclose classified information unless it is done under circumstances which involve what is commonly understood as espionage -- spying for a foreign nation. The government tried, in the prosecution of Daniel Ellsberg, to stretch the espionage statutes to punish his disclosure of the Pentagon Papers, even though he had had no intent to injure the United States, as required by the statute.*

So the secrecy agreement appeared to pose no problem. But what about all the records the CIA had on Bob Vinson and refused to turn over? Of 16 records listed by the CIA, only two were released in full. All or major parts of the rest were kept secret "for reasons of national security." Would they contain anything related to the flight of November 22, 1963? Would they suggest why the CIA forced a man into a job as non-essential as supply supervisor when he was scheduled to retire within 18 months?

Bob wasn't an American James Bond essential for a top-secret mission. There were an awfully lot of supply sergeants in the armed forces, many of whom would have loved to go to work for the CIA. But the CIA insisted on only him. Why?

Hoping to force the CIA to produce Bob's records, Jim filed Bob's affidavit with the Assassination Records Review Board by certified mail on July 22, 1996. The affidavit was received, but (when Jim inquired) he was told it had been lost. A second affidavit was hand carried to the office of the AARB, but no request was ever made to interview Vinson. *And there are no references to Bob Vinson in the ARRB index or in the Board's report.*

It was the beginning of one of the most frustrating periods of Johnston's career. Over the next three years, he did everything he could, turned everywhere he knew for help, certain that those who -- like him -- wanted the truth, would come to his aid just as he had so often come to theirs as an assassination student and ACLU volunteer attorney.

He showed the Vinson video at a national meeting of JFK Lancer Productions in Dallas. Those who viewed it expressed interest and believed Bob to be credible.

He asked for legal help from the ACLU, the Public Citizen Litigation Group, the Assassination Archives and Research Center and from attorneys in Washington D.C. and Florida, where Bob now lived.

He wrote The Assassination Records Review Board, Kansas Senator Pat Roberts (member of the Select Committee on Intelligence), New York Senator Daniel Patrick Moynihan (author of the book *Secrecy*), Vice President Al Gore, the White House, the FBI, the Department of Justice, newspaper editors and television producers asking that they assist in investigating his client and his story.

Those who even responded said basically what came from the Public Citizen Litigation Group -- can't help you and, a bit of advice, no lawsuit to get records from the CIA stands a chance of winning when a "national security" defense is raised.

Those to whom Johnston sent an abstract of Bob's experience, asking for thoughts, ideas, help, names of people who could provide aid were cautious. More than one told Jim that they wished Bob's story didn't take him from Dallas to Roswell, since "Roswell is well known as the location of the alleged flying saucer crash of 1947."

*Flight from Dallas*

Bob Vinson nodded at that sort of response. Everyone who saw flying saucers around CIA bases was crazy. That spared the US government a lot of explaining.

Johnston's correspondence file alone bulged out of a file cabinet drawer -- but only one folder contained any of Bob's redacted records from the CIA gained through the Freedom of Information Act. Finally, it seemed to him, if they couldn't get the full story from the government, that at least they could get their side of the story out to the public.

He told Bob that he thought they'd have to put everything they had into a book and hope they could find a publisher for it. Perhaps through such a book, they could reach others who, like Bob, had information that supplied pieces of the puzzle. And perhaps, together, they could put the puzzle together. Bob agreed, and also agreed that Jon Roe -- whose newspaper and television work he had followed in Wichita -- was the man for the job. A retired prize-winning reporter, who has spoken on and taught journalism throughout the U.S. and abroad, Roe had written 10 books. He cast his first vote for John Kennedy, and had spent much of the 40 years thereafter studying the assassination.

Roe began many interviews with Vinson and Johnston, and also helped with the investigation. The three of them worked in three areas:

1. To establish that the flight took place in a C-54.

2. To establish that the plane had the fuel capacity for such a flight and the ability to land on and take-off from the spot in the Trinity River flood plain Bob had identified.

3. To determine if conspirators had reason and means to be at the Trinity River basin.

If they could do those three things, and supply a credible scenario for the events Bob Vinson experienced that day, it was their hope a publisher would make their findings available to the American public.

What follows is what they learned about the flight from Dallas.

# Chapter 8

# Finding Answers

## The Flight

If the plane took off from Andrews Air Force Base and landed at Roswell, then it should have been logged into the flight logs of those bases for that day. Johnston filed Freedom of Information requests for flight logs from Andrews for November 22, 1963. He was notified by an Air Force spokesman that the logs were destroyed after six months. This differed from the Air Force's earlier reply that they were destroyed after one year.

But, in scouring the report of the Assassination Records Review Board, Roe found a sentence tucked away on page 158: "The only assassination record found was an operations logbook from Andrews Air Force Base that had recorded events at the base on the day of the assassination."

Johnston filed a Freedom of Information inquiry requesting the logbook, and got it. The logbook that could prove Bob's mysterious flight left Andrews the morning of November 22nd. It was all there -- except for one page. The first page. The page that would list morning departures.

Johnston wrote asking why the first page was missing and on September 12, 2000, received a phone call from            at Andrews Air Force Base.        said it was Air Force procedure to dispose of all logbooks after 90 days (not one year as previously reported by the Air Force, or six months as the Air Force reported after that).           said he saw the logbook in a trash container and pulled it out as a momento of the day Kennedy was killed. Page one? He couldn't say. He speculated that it was probably in an earlier log book that was tossed in some other trash container. No doubt, three months, six months or a year after November 22, 1963.

Johnston inquired into this mystery and, on January 12, 2001, received a letter from Don W. Fox, Air Force deputy general counsel, who said the real log book had been destroyed after three months. "Presumeably," Fox wrote, "the reason why you were able to receive copies of the logbook beginning at 1400 hours was because personnel at Andrews Air Force Base Command Post maintained a separate logbook which began when they first learned that President Kennedy had been shot. Given that this second logbook had historical value, it was sent to the National Archives. Accordingly, there are no records to release to you."

He did not explain why Andrews personnel felt it necessary to start a second logbook in addition to the official one.

So no one -- not the Air Force, the CIA or any other agency -- admitted having any record of the C-54's flight. But there was no doubt that the C-54 was one of the CIA's favorite aircraft. After the war, not only the airlines, but the agency had acquired a good many of them for its own use. An example is found in the declassified CIA report on the invasion of Cuba, in which the agency's air force for the invasion was comprised of "16 B-26 light bombers, 10 C-54s and 5 C-46s."[21]

What about the lawyer to whom Bob had told the story back in 1976? He remembered his address, but couldn't quite recall his name. He'd know it if he heard it.

Johnston got the names of all the attorneys who had officed at the address in '76, and Bob identified Lynn D. Allison. Johnston called Allison's office.

He had died in 1999, at age 64.

No one else with whom Bob had spoken that day in 1963 had given a name. Only Bob had given his name when he signed in at Andrews. They had nowhere left to go to find witnesses to the flight.

Well, they had Bobbie on record as having discussed all this with Bob when it happened. And Bob had said he'd told his brother, Paul. Roe called Paul and recorded his statement September 8, 2000. He was impressed by Paul's responses. He didn't volunteer information as people do who are rehearsed. He struggled to recall the incident of 37 years earlier, but -- unaided -- he remembered it. And he remembered something more:

Q: Did Bob seem at all upset when he told you the story?

A: Well, yeah he acted like he thought something might happen to him.

So, 37 years after the flight, all they had was Bob's memory of it and his wife and brother who swore he talked with them about it. And, of course, there was no evidence that the flight didn't take place.

*James P. Johnston & Jon Roe*

## The Fuel Capacity, Landing & Takeoff

Experts contacted by Johnston confirmed that the C-54 could easily make the 1,850 mile trip to Roswell without refueling. The airplane's fuel capacity would take it approximately 3,000 miles.

So the search moved to Dallas, and a long stretch of sand.

Was there a landing space of the type Bob described? And, if there was, could a C-54 land and take off there?

On December 5, 1994, Johnston sent Vinson a 1964 Dallas map and asked him to mark where the plane landed. Bob marked the spot, on the Trinity River Flood Plain just south of downtown Dallas, and Johnston began a search for aerial photos of the area taken around the time of the assassination. While he searched, he wrote retired Colonel L. Fletcher Prouty in Alexandria, Virginia. Prouty had a distinguished Air Force career as liason between the military and the CIA, and is a leading assassination researcher. Although he had gleaned flight information from industry data, Johnston wanted expert opinion from someone who knew the aircraft intimately, and knew what it could do when it had to. May 22, 1997, working from estimates Johnston had made from the map, Prouty wrote: "I see no problem at all with operating a C-54 on and off of a 6,000 foot runway as long as the conditions are 'standard.' Even the 30 foot viaduct would not be a problem under standard conditions" of smooth surface and manageable winds.

After checking with many sources, Jim was able to find and obtain aerial views of the flood plain taken January 4, 1964 by the

U.S. Department of Agriculture. He had them analyzed by Wolf Technical Services, Inc., in Indianapolis, Indiana. In a letter of July 7, 1998, Senior Accident Analyst James S. Sobek reported that analysis of three transparencies of the area revealed:

1. The runway comprised 4,463 feet from Cadiz Street Viaduct on the northwest to Corinth Street Viaduct on the southwest.

2. Corinth Street Vidict was 28 feet above ground surface; Cadiz St. Viadict, 23 feet above ground surface.

3. The ground surface had no substantial bumps, slopes or steep elevation changes.

There was the runway. About 1,500 feet shorter than the one Prouty said would cause "no problem at all" with a smooth runway and good weather.

Johnston searched all over the country for weather data, and ended up in correspondence with Texas State Climatologist John F. Griffiths at Texas A&M in College Station. June 16, 1997, Griffith's sent data showing that from 2:00 to 6:00 P.M., the wind was out of the NW or WNW at from 19 to 23 knots -- near ideal conditions.

Then, August 16, 1998, Johnston read a front page story in his local newspaper -- *The Wichita Eagle* -- in which Major William Hendrix, USAF (Retired) recalled flying missions in the 1948-49 Berlin Airlift. He spent more than 525 hours at the controls of the C-54 on 125 missions. Here was a man who would know first-hand what the aircraft could do.

Maj. Hendrix responded to Jim's letter August 27: "We could do things with the 54 that couldn't be done with many others."

"Even with a total weight of 68-70,000 pounds, we could land at Templehof airfield in Berlin on what had been an ME-109 fighter base. The main runway was 5,000 feet long. We had no trouble at all in landing or braking. I did not take off from Templehof fully loaded but we did so from Rhein Maine air base, and, yes, in less that 6,000 feet. Believe it or not, some of the 54's would become airborne in 4500-5500 feet, depending on which engines they had. Engine power was either 1350 or 1450 horsepower."

"Take-off performance from Templehof, when empty, was FUN. We would place the nose wheel at the very beginning of the runway and lock the brakes. Twenty degrees of flaps and full power, release brakes and pull the control column into your gut. We were off the ground at the *third* runway light."

Did that mean the plane could take off from the 4,463-foot flood plain runway? Johnston wrote, giving the conditions and asking that question.

July 15, 1999, Maj. Hendrix replied: "it is my personal opinion that a C-54 could easily have landed in the Trinity Flood Plain and have taken off therefrom, the depicted area."

So the landing and takeoff at the spot pointed out by Bob were perfectly within the aircraft's capabilities.

## Who Was on the Airplane

Two men in the cockpit and two who scrambled aboard and sat in the front of the cabin. Who were they?

First, the official reaction.

The White House e-mail from Johnston was sent to the FBI, which wrote telling Johnston to contact the Dallas office with the informaton. He did, and he got back a response from Wilbur M. Gregory, Jr., Chief Division Counsel on December 2, 1998, which said:

*While we do not contest Mr. Vinson's observations, we must note that many individuals reported seeing "Oswald look-a-likes" during the period surrounding the assassination. Moreover, without specific information such as flight manifests, passenger lists and the like, it is unlikely that we would be able to ascertain the name of the passenger(s). While Mr. Vinson's recollections are interesting, there are no new allegations which would warrant further scrutiny by this office.*

Indeed many individuals reported seeing "Oswald look-a-likes," for a good reason. "Lee Harvey Oswald" was all over Dallas just before the shooting -- in so many places at once that there could only have been look-a-likes on the scene. At the very least, one look-a-like.

Many assassination researchers have documented sightings and evidence that more than one person claiming to be Lee Oswald was in Dallas before the president's murder. One was Carl Oglesby, author of *The Yankee and Cowboy War*:

*There is evidence actually of several Oswalds in circulation at this time. There is in the first place the presumptive original himself installed since late October in the depository. There is the thirty-five-year old Oswald in Mexico City freshening up the red spoor at the Cuban and Soviet missions. There is the Oswald or Oswalds who move around Dallas just before the hit planting unforgettable memories of a man about to become an assassin: the Oswald of the firing range who fires cross-range into other people's targets and then belligerently starts a loud argument in which he carefully and loudly repeats his name; the Oswald of the used-car lot who sneers at Texas and the American flag and drives recklessly, though Oswald had no driver's license and did not know how to drive; the Oswald who visited exile Sylvia Odio a few weeks before the assassination in the company of two anti-Castro militants at a time when the REAL Oswald (or is it the other way around?) was supposed to be in Mexico City. Who are all these Oswalds?"* [22]

In his book, *Conspiracy*, Anthony Summers devotes much time to what appear to be carefully orchestrated appearances by someone claiming to be Oswald calling attention to himself. He writes:

*Predictably the Kennedy assassination sparked off literally hundreds of "Oswald" sightings, and most would eventually be discounted. Others, however, were strikingly different -- both because of the obvious integrity of the witness reporting and because of the credible detail they provided. These cases worried official investigators but eventually were discarded like jigsaw pieces that get into the wrong box.*

But, like so many researchers who have rediscovered and re-investigated these sightings, Summers reached the conclusion that someone may well have been impersonating Oswald "either to incriminate him or to confuse later investigation or both."

*Flight from Dallas*

The first of more than a dozen sightings compiled by Summers was just a little over two months before the assassination, September 25, 1963, when a young man entered the Austin Selective Service System offices, identified himself as Harvey Oswald and asked the assistant chief of the administrative division what she could do to get his "other than honorable conditions" Marine Corps discharge upgraded based on two years subsequent good conduct. He said the blemish on his record kept him from getting a job. The assistant chief -- Mrs. Lee Dannelly -- couldn't find him in her files, and suggested he try the Fort Worth offices, where he said he was then living. He thanked her and left.

But that day, September 25, Oswald was in New Orleans, setting off for a well-documented trip to Mexico that would take him nowhere near Austin, Texas.

Such was the mild-mannered and polite "Oswald," who would be recalled by a draft official two months later. But other appearances by the other Oswald were louder and more abusive, seemingly aimed at making a distinctive impression in the more crowded commercial marketplace.

Typical of those was the "Lee Oswald" who told salesmen in a Dallas car showroom on November 9 that he would receive "a lot of money in the next two or three weeks." Still the high prices on cars led him to state he might have to go "back to Russia where they treat workers like men." He then took one of the salesmen on a demonstration drive, careening through Dallas at speeds up to 80 miles per hour. All this despite the fact that the real Lee Oswald couldn't drive and had no driver's license. In spite of the three witnesses to his visit, the Warren Commission disregarded the evidence "on the usual ground that other evidence placed the real Oswald elsewhere."

Dozens of times during the days before the assassination, a man witnesses describe as looking like Lee Harvey Oswald attracts attention throughout the area. As New Orleans District Attorney Jim Garrison and his investigators concluded: "A trail of phony incriminating evidence had been carefully laid down prior to the execution of the President, leading to Oswald as the scapegoat."

Bizarre? Not to those who worked in the CIA. To them it was standard operating procedure, as Terry Reed and John Cummings point out in their book *Compromised: Clinton, Bush And The CIA*. In their report on how arms were illegally supplied to El Salvador by the Reagan administration, they point out that the CIA supplied "two of everything" so that operatives could use, for instance, a second airplane as a "decoy operation" that gave plotters "the ability to appear to be in two places at the same time."[23]

A double, showing up throughout the Dallas area before the assassination, drawing attention to himself, and most often accompanied by others -- particularly one man described as "Cuban." Leaving a trail that pointed to the patsy Oswald, and then participating in the assassination, such a double would be invaluable before the killing, and would have to be invisible immediately after it.

*Flight from Dallas*

And apparently, that invisibility would be achieved and maintained at all costs, including ignoring eyewitnesses and changing some of their reports.

Prime example of that is Julia Ann Mercer, who -- caught in a traffic jam on Elm Street an hour before the assassination -- was stopped beside a pickup truck that was parked part-way up on the curb. She watched a young man carrying a rifle in a "not too well concealed covering" leave the passenger side of the truck and climb up the steep incline onto the grassy knoll. In addition, she later positively identified the truck's driver as Jack Ruby. After the assassination, Mercer reported what she had seen to the Dallas Sheriff's office and the FBI, but she was never called as a witness by the Warren Commission. Thus no one ever got a description (let alone a positive identification) of just who she saw carry a rifle up the grassy knoll from which scores of witnesses said shots were fired minutes later.

Jim Garrison's book, *On the Trail of the Assassins*, is one of several that list such witnesses as:

Railroad yard switchman Lee Bowers who -- from the railroad's 14-foot high glassed-in tower -- watched two men standing behind the picket fence on the knoll watching the approaching parade. Earlier he had seen a man driving around in the railroad yard behind the man appearing to speak into a hand-held microphone.

Union Terminal Railroad's signal supervisor S.M. Holland who "counted four shots and…in this group of trees…there was a shot, a report. I don't know whether it was a shot. I can't say that, and a puff of smoke came out about six or eight feet above the ground right out from under those trees....I have no doubt about seeing that puff of smoke come out from under those trees....I definitely saw the puff of smoke and heard the report...."[24]

Holland wasn't alone. Several witnesses heard shots coming from the picket fence on the grassy knoll, and smoke rising from the cluster of trees. And even more said they saw men running from the knoll after the shooting into the railroad yard, from which there was easy exit to the nearby floodplain where the airplane carrying Bob Vinson landed.

In *The Fourth Decade,* a journal of JFK assassination research, Grant Leitma reports that: "Gordon Arnold, a young army soldier, wanted to get a good view of the motorcade in order to use his movie camera. As he approached the overpass bridge, he was rebuffed by a plain clothes man identifying himself as CIA. AP photographer James Altgens was also denied permission to be on the bridge. Was this unidentified CIA (?) man assigned to keep people away from the N.W. corner of the grassy knoll concealing the sniper(s)?"

Arnold went on to tell *The Dallas Morning News* that the first shot went by his left ear, and the next shot passed over him as he hit the dirt. Then, he said, a man in a policeman's uniform ran up to him, kicked him and ripped the film from his camera.[25]

In all, witnesses heard from four to six shots that day. One man was struck by part of a bullet fired from behind Kennedy. Other witnesses said they saw a shot strike the pavement directly in front of the President's car and ricochet into the car's windshield. Another shot, from behind, entered the president's back and is alleged to be the bullet that fell out onto the stretcher on which he was taken into Parkland Hospital. That allegation is virtually impossible, since the bullet is virtually pristine.

The effects of two frontal shots were witnessed not just during the attack, but afterwards at Parkland Hospital, where testimony and written medical records of doctors and staff corroborate that all were convinced of a right parietal headshot and that the neck wound was a perfect entrance wound before doctors ripped it open for a tracheotomy.

There is also substantial evidence that autopsy photos of the front of Kennedy's head wound were suppressed and altered to hide the fact that it was an entry wound. The report of the Assassination Records Review Board cites considerable evidence of tampering with the autopsy report, and substitution of phony head wound photos for the real ones.

The Board's investigative staff located witness Saundraw Spencer, who worked at the Naval Photographic Center in 1963. Spencer testified under oath that she developed post-mortem photos of Kennedy in November that were different from those identified as Kennedy's that had been in the National Archives since 1966.[26]

In the video, *The Men Who Killed Kennedy*, Lt. Col. Dan Marvin -- veteran of eight combat campaigns and for 15 years a paratrooper in the Green Berets -- says that he took guerilla training at Fort Bragg, North Carolina, where the group studied the JFK assassination as the perfect plan using Oswald as the patsy. The implication was strong, he says, that the CIA had been involved in the assassination.

August 1, 1965, Lt. Marvin says, he was asked by his superiors to do a hit on Lieutenant Commander William Bruce Pitzer at Bethesda Naval Hospital. Pitzer, he was told, took photos during the Kennedy autopsy that prove a frontal head shot. Marvin refused because it would have required a domestic killing. He claims Captain David H. Vanuck accepted the assignment. Pitzer's shooting death October 29, 1966 was ruled a suicide, even though the left-handed Pitzer was shot by a handgun in the right side of his head. Years later, when Marvin tried to locate Vanuck, the Army told him no Vanuck had ever served in the U.S. Army.[27]

The U.S. government refuses to show Pitzer's family a copy of his autopsy report.[28]

So it seems probable that one or more assassins fired from in front of the motorcade.

How did they get away? The quickest and easiest route was to hop into a vehicle and drive right out of the railroad yard less than a mile to the floodplain. Johnston came to this conclusion after spending time in Dallas checking out all the various theories, and in the process, disproving one that had sounded oh so perfect.

That was the storm sewer escape route.

Since there were storm sewer openings at the top and the bottom of the grassy knoll, some had speculated that shooters had been hidden in those openings, fired the fatal shots and then escaped through the sewer system.

It was a perfect match with Bob's two mysterious figures and the plane pickup. Especially since the storm sewer opening is on Industrial Boulevard, only 1,500 feet southwest of the assassination site, running southeast along the north bank of the Trinity River to the airplane's landing site between Corinth and Cadiz. It had also been reported that a researcher had walked from the Dealy Plaza sewer opening to the Trinity River at Industrial Park in just 27 minutes.

The fitting and perfect escape route. Except for the fact that it's impossible.

Johnston investigated those sewer openings with Patrick Pippin, RPLS, assistant chief city surveyor for the City of Dallas. Among other things, they found that the opening at the top of the knoll behind the picket fence is seven feet deep. No one but a giant could stand in it and shoot a rifle at the approaching motorcade. The lower opening at Elm Street and the sewer line to the flood plain is no more than 15 inches wide, and goes away from, not toward the flood plain, making a crawl to the pickup area impossible.

No, both Pippin and Johnston were convinced no one could have shot and slithered away through those sewer lines. The chances are far better they were instead the men seen by several witnesses preparing to fire and then leaving the railroad yard. They would have attracted no special attention leaving that area in a regular vehicle and later transferring to a maintenance type jeep, driving the few blocks on Industrial Boulevard and waiting at the construction site where the Oswald double and his Cuban keeper boarded the C-54 and were never seen or heard from again after the plane landed at Roswell AFB.

## Chapter 9

# The Scenario of an Assassination

Friday morning, November 22, 1963, Dallas: Two men (a tall Cuban and a shorter Caucasian) arrive at the grassy knoll about an hour before President Kennedy's motorcade is scheduled to drive by. One is dropped off in front of the knoll in a car driven by Jack Ruby and climbs the knoll carrying a rifle. The other arrives at the knoll from the back, driven into the railroad yard that stretches behind the picket fence on the knoll. He's dropped off by the driver who waits in the vehicle amidst the other cars. The shooters take their positions, while others keep onlookers away from their lair. One or two others take up their positions to the north (which will be behind the motorcade).

Washington D.C.: Following orders, two CIA pilots ready their aircraft at Andrews Air Force Base for a flight to Denver. When they board the plane, they find an Air Force sergeant on board. They say nothing to him. He must be there for a reason, and they know better than to ask questions.

In Dallas, two shots from behind Kennedy strike the president in the back and in the back of the head. Two shots from in front strike him in the throat and (the fatal shot) in the right side of the head. Two more shots miss the president altogether.

Above Nebraska, one of the pilots gives the sergeant information he assumes the sergeant needs. Over the intercom he says that the president was shot at 12:29. Bob Vinson gets that information one minute after the act. Even though the shooting is officially listed as occurring at 12:30, eye-witnesses say a large clock in Dealy Plaza read 12:29. At 12:30, no one outside the presidential limo knows Kennedy has been hit. But those in the airplane over Nebraska knew.

Immediately, the pilots turn away from their alleged Denver destination towards Dallas. Either they had orders to do so when they got word of the shooting, or those orders came with news of the shooting. Their orders say nothing of the Air Force sergeant. They believe he is there -- as are they -- to do a specific job about which they don't need to know -- indeed, are better off not knowing -- anything.

Having shot the president, the two frontal assassins walk back from the fence, get into the vehicle and are driven away from Dealy Plaza to wait in a jeep at the flood plain construction site for the C-54.

There are reports of a mysterious plane or planes leaving Dallas throughout the afternoon and evening hours of November 22nd. The plane with Bob Vinson aboard lands where it was sent, the shooters climb aboard, and speak to no one. The plane lands at Roswell, and the four leave headed toward another rendezvous, leaving the mysterious sergeant aboard.

Not until long after November 22nd, when one or more of those four are debriefed, does the subject of the sergeant come up. No one knows who he was or what he was doing there. A check up and down the chain of command results in consternation, concern and then panic.

Find him, the word goes out. And, finally, the sign-in sheet at the flight counter at Andrews Air Force Base shows that Robert K. Vinson signed up looking for a flight to Colorado.

And so it is that six months after the assassination, agents are all over Colorado Springs asking questions about Bob and Bobbie Vinson, who were then each forced to sign personal detailed history statements and confidentiality agreements. What happens to Bob Vinson? Well, he sat through it all and hasn't murmured a word about it. That seems to show he's either a Kennedy hater or looking after his own hide. He certainly is a mild-mannered sort. Not a trouble-maker. So, co-opt him. Put him to work for the CIA, pay him well, and keep a close watch on him.

They did. And through it all, he was a model of propriety.

Until now.

It's right out of an Alfred Hitchcock movie. An average, law-abiding citizen lands in the middle of a conspiracy of the highest order. And when he tries to find the truth, he's told it never happened. The CIA won't let go of all his records. The Air Force has no record of his flight. And, of course, the Warren Commission says that John F. Kennedy was killed by a lone, crazed assassin.

# Chapter 10
# A Patriot's Questions

The rain has cleared and the sun is now bathing west Florida in an early afternoon sauna. Used to the heat and humidity, Bob Vinson leads his visitors from one giant airplane to another, explaining in his soft drawl why and when each was built, and how it was used by the U.S. Air Force. He's excited by every visit he makes to the Eglin Air Force Base Flight Museum. He's proud of his military service. He's happy about the life he and Bobbie now live. But he still seeks confirmation of his belief that his country will and can provide him the answers to the questions he's carried with him for 40 years. He still cannot believe it would not.

"I'm not what you would call an assassination buff," he says. "But I do believe there was some kind of conspiracy. Every time I'd see an article on the assassination, I stop and wonder if I have the answer to this puzzle. Could this small piece of information fit into the larger picture to help us learn what happened? It would be good to know who did it. The government? Cuba? The Mafia? The CIA? Whoever caused it should have to pay for it, you know? It worries me that someone could do it and get away with it. Can they do something that big and get away with it? If they can, we've got to stop it. And if I have one little piece of information, I need to share it."

It's Bob's hope that someone who reads this book will have another bit of information to put with his and all the other bits. It's his hope that there's still time to solve the puzzle and answer the questions.

The mystery of the 20th century may still be solved by everyday Americans who come together in the 21st century, each with a small party of the puzzle.

He hopes that -- if you are one of those Americans who has knowledge of a piece of the puzzle -- you'll contact Jim Johnston, and add it to the jigsaw puzzle they work on daily, the puzzle they'll never give up trying to solve. Johnston's address is: P.O. Box 3089, Wichita, KS 67201. His e-mail address is: Zapatajpj@aol.com. He works with Robert Vinson in hopes of disproving the suggestion of Victor Marchetti in the introduction to his book, *The CIA and the Cult of Intelligence:*

*It has been said that among the dangers faced by a democratic society in fighting totalitarian systems, such as fascism and communism, is that the democratic government runs the risk of imitating its enemies' methods and, thereby, destroying the very democracy that it is seeking to defend. I cannot help wondering if my government is more concerned with defending our democratic system or more intent upon imitating the methods of totalitarian regimes in order to maintain its already inordinate power over the American people.* [29]

Such things are possible. Indeed, forces high in our government may have carried out a coup d'état and covered it up. But anything that is covered up can be uncovered, indeed must be uncovered if America is to remain a true democracy.

That is why America produces men like Bob Vinson and Jim Johnston. And men like John Kennedy, who said:

*A man does what he must -- in spite of personal consequences, in spite of obstacles and dangers -- and this is the basis of all human morality.*

# INDEX

A-12, 67
ACLU, 76, 84
Air Force One, 31
Allen, Mark, 74
Allison, Lynn D., 89
Altgens, James, 98
Andrews Air Force Base, 21, 22, 33, 68, 81, 87, 88, 89, 103, 105
Armentrout, Sgt., 66, 68
Arnold, Gordon, 98
Assassination Archives & Research Center, 84
Assassination Records Review Board (AARB), 72, 74, 83, 84, 87, 99
Associated Press (AP), 27, 28, 98
Atomic Energy Commission, 66, 67, 82
Aurora, The, 67
Austin Selective Service System Office, 95
Autopsy report, JFK, 99
B2 Stealth Bomber, 67
Baker, Bobby, 18
Barkley, Alben W., 12
Bay of Pigs, 17
Berlin Airlift, 91
Bethesda Naval Hospital, 100
Blackbird SR, 67, 68
Bowers, Lee
Bundy, McGeorge, 31
Bush, President George H.W., 72

C-54, vii, 1, 22, 49, 68, 85, 88, 90, 91, 92, 101, 104
Camp Kilmer, NJ, 10
Central Intelligence Agency (CIA), 11, 12, 14, 17, 18, 27, 30, 34, 35, 55, 63, 66, 68, 69, 71, 74, 78, 80, 81, 82, 83, 84, 85, 88, 90, 96, 98, 100, 103, 105, 106, 107, 117
Chapman, Col., 20
*CIA and the Cult of Intelligence, The*, 82, 107, 117
Cold War, The, 10, 77
Cole, Capt. Robert E. 32, 33
*Colorado Springs Gazette*, 38
Colorado Springs, CO, 1, 19, 21, 22, 25, 28, 32, 36, 38, 82, 105
*Compromised Clinton, Bush and the CIA*, 96
*Conspiracy*, 94
Corbin, Noah, 13
Cuba missile crisis, 17
Cuban, 26, 101, 103
Cummings, John, 96

Dallas, 1, 2, 20, 21, 25, 36, 49, 50, 71, 74, 75, 78, 84, 86, 90, 93, 94, 95, 96, 97, 98, 100, 101, 103, 104
*Dallas Morning News*, 98
Dallas Sheriff's Office, 97
Dannelly, Mrs. Lee, 95
Dealy Plaza, 70, 101, 104
Department of Justice, 84
Depression, The, 4
Dewey, Gov. Thomas E., 12, 14
Douglas Aircraft, 23
Dulles, Allen, 10, 12, 14, 18

Eisenhower, Pres. Dwight D., 13, 14
Eglin Air Force Base Flight Museum, 106
Ellsberg, Daniel, 83
Enewetak Island, 13

109

Federal Bureau of Investigation (FBI), 32, 65, 71, 84, 93, 97
Flight of November, 68, 79, 83
Florala, Alabama, 5, 6
Ford, Pres. Gerald, 71
Fort Bragg, NC, 99
Fort Myer Army Base, VA, 33, 35, 36
*Fourth Decade, The*, 98
Fox, Donald W., 88
Freedom of Information Act (FOIA), 63, 81, 85

Garrison, Jim, 70, 96, 97
Glickman, Rep. Dan, 73
Gore, Vice-Pres. Al, 84
Grable, Major, 32
grassy knoll, 97, 98, 100, 103
Green Berets, 99
Gregory Jr., Wilbur M., 93
Griffiths, John F., 91

Hatteburg, Larry, vii, 73, 74, 78, 79, 80
Hendrix, Major William, USAF (Ret.), vii, 91, 92
Hitchcock, Alfred, 105
Holland, S. M., 97, 98
Hoover, J. Edgar, 32
House Armed Services Committee, 3, 20, 43
House Select Committee on Intelligence, 71, 84
HQUSAF, 33
Huddleston Vinson, Roberta, 2, 19, 20, 21, 25, 28, 29, 30, 32, 33, 34, 37, 38, 66, 69, 70, 71, 72, 73, 78, 79, 82, 89, 106
Hydrogen Bomb, 13

JFK, 71, 74, 84, 98, 99, 117

JFK Lancer Productions, 84
Johnson, Lyndon B., 18, 30, 32
Johnson, Major James W., 12
*Johnston Report, The*, 76
Johnston Sloan, Casey, vii, 78
Johnston, James P., vii, 76, 77, 78, 79, 80, 81, 82, 83, 84, 85, 87, 88, 89, 90, 91, 92, 93, 100, 101, 107, 108

KAKETV, 73, 74
Kansas Newman College, 13
Kennedy, John F., vii, 4, 5, 6, 9, 13, 14, 15, 16, 17, 18, 20, 28, 30, 31, 70, 71, 73, 74, 76, 77, 78, 80, 85, 88, 94, 98, 99, 100, 103, 104, 105, 108, 117
Choate School, 4
death, 28, 77
declassification of records, 74
election to Congress, 9, 13
firing of Dulles and CIA staff, 18
marriage to Jacqueline Bouvier, 14
Navy & Marine Corp. medal, 6
*New Frontier* speech, 16
political career, 9, 13, 14, 16
*Profiles in Courage*, 14
Pulitzer Prize, 14
speech at American University, 77
*Why England Slept*, 5

Lane, Mark, 31
Langley, VA, 14, 34, 63
Las Vegas, NV, 38, 54, 66, 68, 69, 81
Leitma, Grant, 98
Lindsey, Gorman, 6, 7
Lockhart, AL, 5, 11, 34
Lodge, Henry Cabot, 30

Lowry Air Force Base, 22, 26

Mafia, the, 106
Marchetti, Victor, 82, 107
Mark Allen, 74
Marks, John D., 82, 117
Marvin, Lt. Col. Dan, 99, 100
McDaniel Motor Co., 5
*Men Who Killed Kennedy, The*, 99
Mercer, Julia Ann, 97
Mobley, West, Jennings and Shaw, 70
Moynihan, Sen. Daniel Patrick, 84

Naha Air force Base, Okinawa, 15
National Archives, 88, 99
National Security Act Memorandum #263, 18
National Security Council, 11
Naval Photographic Center, 99
Navy & Marine Corp Medal, 6
Nebraska, 24, 103
Nellis mountain range, 67
New Mexico, 1, 27, 67
NORAD, 19, 33, 45
Nuclear Test Ban Treaty, 18

Odio, Sylvia, 94
Oglesby, Carl, 93
Okinawa, 13, 15, 41
Oswald, Lee Harvey, 29, 31, 32, 78, 93, 94, 95, 96, 100, 101

Parkland Hospital, 99
Peck, Gregory, 12
Penrose, Helen Mary, 10, 12, 14
*Pentagon Papers, The*, 83
Personal History Statement, 32, 33, 82
Pippin, Patrick, vii, 101
Pitzer, Lt. Com. William Bruce, 100

Powers, Frances Gary, 68
Prouty, Col. L. Fletcher, 90, 91
PT 109, 6
Public Citizen Litigation Group, 84
Purple Heart, 6

Rankin, H. Lee, 30, 31
Reed, Terry, 96
Rhein Maine Air Base, 92
Roberts, Kansas Sen. Pat, 84
Roe, Jon, 85, 87, 89
Roosevelt, Pres. Franklin Delano, 77
Roswell Air Force Base, 27, 102
Roswell, NM, 27, 28, 37, 67, 84, 87, 90, 102, 104
Ruby, Jack, 31, 97, 103
*Rush to Judgement*, 31, 117
Rusk, Dean, 30

*Secrecy*, 33, 35, 84
Secrecy Agreement, 33, 35, 69, 74, 82, 83
Senate Armed Services Committee, 10
Shaw, Clay, 70
Site 51, 55, 67
Smathers, Sen. George, 18
Sobek, James S., vii, 61, 91
Spencer, Saundraw, 99
Stealth Fighter F-117, 67
Stone, Oliver, 71
storm sewer escape route, 100, 101
Summers, Anthony, 94, 95

Templehof Airfield, 92
Texas, 14, 15, 19, 21, 91, 94, 95
Texas A&M, 91
timetable, assassination, 103, 104
Trinity River and flood plain, 25, 86, 90, 92, 98, 100, 101, 104

Truman, Pres. Harry S., 9, 10, 12, 44
*Twelve O'Clock High*, 12

U2 spy plane, 67, 68
UFOs, 27, 67
US Air Force, vii, 1, 2, 11, 12, 13, 14, 16, 19, 21, 22, 23, 24, 25, 31, 32, 33, 34, 37, 66, 69, 81, 87, 88, 90, 91, 103, 104, 105, 106
US Department of Agriculture, 91

Vanuck, Capt. David H., 100
Vietnam, 18, 30
Vinson, Carl, 3, 20, 43
Vinson, Chief Justice Fred, 4, 14, 20, 44
   appointment to Supreme Court, 44
   death, 14
Vinson, Robert, vii, 2, 3, 4, 5, 6, 7, 8, 9, 10, 11, 12, 13, 14, 15, 16, 17, 19, 20, 21, 22, 23, 24, 25, 26, 27, 28, 29, 30, 32, 33, 34, 35, 36, 37, 38, 39, 40, 41, 42, 43, 44, 45, 47, 48, 57, 66, 67, 68, 69, 70, 71, 72, 73, 74, 76, 78, 79, 80, 81, 82, 83, 84, 85, 86, 87, 89, 90, 92, 93, 98, 101, 103, 104, 105, 106, 107, 108
   Air Force enlistment, 11
      Andrews Air Force Base, 21, 22, 33, 68, 81, 87, 88, 89, 103, 105
      Ent Air force Base, 19, 21, 22, 32, 33, 37
      Nellis Air Force Base, 67, 81
   Army enlistment, 6, 7
      Barksdale Air Force Base, 8
      Camp Polk, LA, 7, 8, 9
      Fort Dix, NJ, 9
   at the Pentagon, 20, 21
   birth, 3
   contact with James P. Johnston, 75, 78, 79, 80
   contact with Larry Hatteburg, 73, 74
   daughters, 12, 14
   education, 12, 13
   Elgin Air Force Base, 11, 12, 106
   employment as city administrator, 2, 70
   family, 3, 4, 6, 7
   fear of government reprisal, 74, 80
   Florala, Alabama, 5, 6
   marriage to Helen Penrose, 10
   marriage to Roberta Huddleston, 14
   medals & citations, 47, 69
   psychological testing by CIA, 34, 35
   retirement to Florida, 80
   US Government Training Program, 11
Vinson, Roberta Huddleston (Bobbie), 2, 19, 20, 21, 25, 28, 29, 30, 32, 33, 34, 37, 38, 66, 69, 70, 71, 72, 73, 78, 79, 82, 89, 106

Warren Commission, 30, 32, 37, 70, 72, 77, 96, 97, 105
Warren, Chief Justice Earl, 12, 13, 30
Washington, DC, 13, 20, 31, 33, 34, 37, 69, 84, 103
White House, 17, 30, 31, 84, 93
*Wichita Eagle, The*, 91
Wichita, KS, 13, 70, 71, 72, 73, 76, 85, 107
Wolf Technical Services, 91

*Flight from Dallas*

*Yankee and Cowboy War, The*, 93         Zapruder film, 70

*James P. Johnston & Jon Roe*

# About The Authors

James P. Johnston is a practicing attorney in Wichita, Kansas and for many years has served as a volunteer attorney for the American Civil Liberties Union.

Jon Roe is an independent award-winning journalist in Wichita, Kansas who has written numerous books and articles. He recently retired from The Wichita Eagle, a Knight Ridder publication.

# END NOTES

[1] Marchetti, Victor and John D. Marks, *The CIA and the Cult of Intelligence* (Knopf, New York, 1974) p. 273.

[1] Ibid

[2] Lane, Mark, *Plausible Denial* (Thunder's Mouth Press, New York. 1991), p. 41.

[3] Ibid

[4] Marchetti and Marks, pp. 305-306.

[5] *New York Times*, April 25, 1966, p. 10, col. 3.

[6] Salandria, Vincent J., The Assassination of President John F. Kennedy: A Model of Explanation, *Computers and Automation*, December, 1971 & January, 1972, p. 82.

[7] Ibid, p. 85

[8] Ibid

[9] Benson, Michael, *Who's Who in the JFK Assassination* (Citadel, Secaucus, N.J., 1993) p. 24.

[10] Schlesinger, Arthur M., Jr., *Robert Kennedy and His Times* (Ballantine Books, New York, 1978) p. 783

[11] *New York Times*, January 2, 1964, p. 7.

[12] Lane, Mark, p. 41

[13] Lane, Mark, *Rush to Judgement* (Fawcett, New York, 1967) quoting the January 11, 1964 *New York Times*, pp. 309-310.

[14] Salandria, pp. 7-8.

[15] Cornwell, Gary, *Real Answers* (Paleface Press, Spicewood, Texas, 1998) pp. 159-160.

[16] Marchetti & Marks, p. 273.

[17] Scott, Peter Dale, *Deep Politics and the Death of JFK* (University of California Press, 1993) p. 21.

[18] *Area 51: The Real Story,* Discovery Channel.

[19] Ibid.

[20] *Final Report of the Assassination Records Review Board* (Washington D.C., 1998) p. 8.

[21] Kornbluh, Peter, ed. *Bay of Pigs Declassified: The Secret CIA Report on the Invasion of Cuba,Ó (*1998, National Security Archive, Annex C) pp. 118-119.

[22] Oglesby, Carl, *The Yankee and Cowboy War* (Berkley Medallion, 1977) pp. 107-108.

[23] Reed, Terry and Cummings, John, *Compromised* (SPI Books, New York) pp. 95-96.

[24] Garrison, p16

[25] Benson, p. 22

[26] *Final Report of the Assassination Records Review Board,* p. 122.

[27] *The Men Who Killed Kennedy,* video shown on the Discovery Channel.

[28] Benson, p. 363

[29] Marchetti, p. 2

Lightning Source UK Ltd.
Milton Keynes UK
UKOW02f1930091215

264451UK00001B/281/P